The Real Musashi

Also by William de Lange

Miyamoto Musashi: A Life in Arms
The Real Musashi, I, II
Famous Japanese Swordsmen, I, II, III
A History of Japanese Journalism
A Dictionary of Japanese Proverbs
A Dictionary of Japanese Idioms
Pars Japonica
Iaido

Available in eBooks

The Real Musashi, I, II, III
Famous Samurai: Kamiizumi Nobutsuna
Famous Samurai: Yagyū Munenori
Famous Samurai: Ono Tadaaki
Through the Eye of the Needle (Pars Japonica)

Available in Apps

A Dictionary of Japanese Proverbs
A Dictionary of Japanese Idioms

THE REAL MUSASHI
Origins of a Legend III

A Miscellany

TRANSLATED AND ANNOTATED BY WILLIAM DE LANGE

TOYO PRESS

For more on books by William de Lange visit:

www.williamdelange.com

First edition, 2016

Published by TOYO Press

Copyright © 2016 by William de Lange.

Protected by copyright under the terms of the International Copyright Union; all rights reserved. Except for fair use in book reviews, no part of this book may be reproduced for any reason by any means, including any method of photographic reproduction, without the permission of the publisher.

Printed in the U.S.A.

ISBN 978-1-891640-86-5

Library of Congress Cataloging-in-Publication data available

For Joris van Nispen

Table of Contents

Introduction ix

❂ Early Edo Texts 1653–96

The *Tomari Jinja munefuda*	3
The *Kokura hibun*	8
The *Sōkyū-sama o-degatari*	15
The *Hayashi Razan bunshū*	21
The *Kaijō monogatari*	24
The *Numata kaki*	31
The *Yoshioka-den*	33
The *Hōkōsho*	39

❂ Mid-Edo Texts 1704–9

The *Kōkai fūhansō*	45
The *Watanabe Kōan taiwa-ki*	51
The *Honchō bugei shoden*	55
The *Bushō kanjō-ki*	64
The *Dōbō goen*	66
The *Koro usawa*	69
The *Kōkō zatsuroku*	71
The *Harima kagami*	77

The *Mukashibanashi*	*82*
The *Seiryūwa*	*85*
The *Saiyū zakki*	*88*
The *Gekken sōdan*	*91*

❧ Late Edo, Meiji Texts 1851–97

The *Tōsakushi*	*98*
The *Mimasaka ryakushi*	*120*
The *Bisan hōkan*	*124*
Old Provinces	*130*
Castles, Temples, and Shrines	*132*
Important Castles	*141*
Important Temples	*143*
Important Shrines	*144*
Historical Periods	*145*
Battles and Rebellions	*146*
Glossary	*147*
Bibliography	*150*
Index	*154*

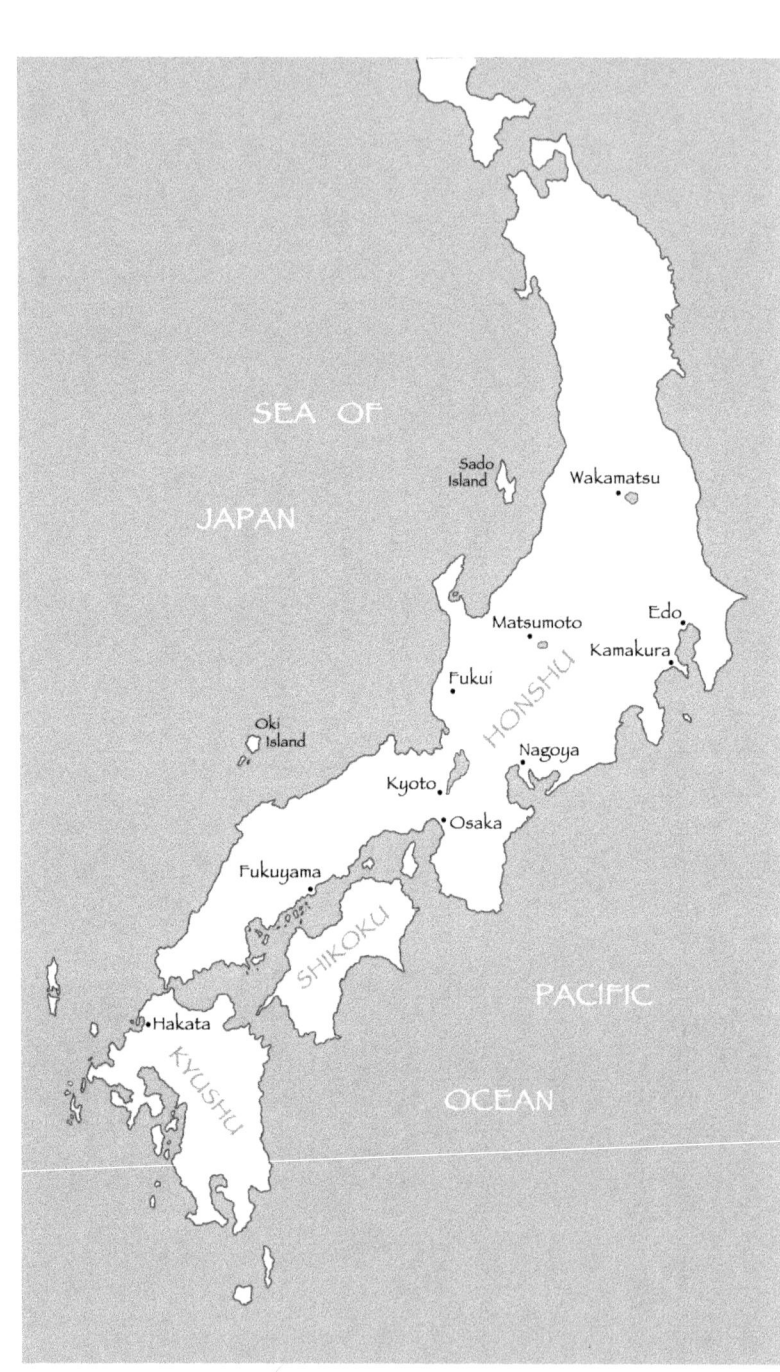

Introduction

The Legend of Miyamoto Musashi

No swordsman in Japanese history is so revered and celebrated as Miyamoto Musashi. In Japan alone close to a thousand works have taken Musashi as their subject, many in the form of novels, the first one appearing as far back as the turn of the eighteenth century. Even now, more than four and a half centuries after his last exploits, hardly a year passes by without the lone swordsman turning up in some newly released film or television adaptation.

Sadly, amid this veritable deluge of books, comics, films, television soaps, and docudramas, little room is given to the old histories, topographies, and memoirs written by men who, though they may not have known Musashi alive, faithfully recorded what had been passed down by men who had. This is especially the case since most of what is known about Musashi today is based on the vivid recollections of these very men. Their value is increased by Musashi's own reticence about his exploits, to which, in his *Gorin no sho* (*Book of Five Rings*), he dedicates no more than a few paragraphs.

Given Musashi's huge popularity, many of the more human aspects of this medieval warrior have with time been relegated to the margins in favor of a highly polished portrayal of his undisputed fencing skills. The resulting image is one of an invincible war-machine, a two-dimensional and hollow caricature, bereft of the personal traits that make us all human.

It is all the more exciting, then, to return to these earliest of records to find behind the myth a man of real flesh, who in spite of his unparalleled mastery of the sword has all the traits and idiosyncrasies to which all of us are prone. We discover that he was an extraordinarily precocious youth who had a deeply troubled relationship with his father. That background, combined with his rather disheveled physical appearance, may well have been the driving forces behind his desire to impress his friends in youth and champion over his adversaries when he reached adulthood. We discover that in old age he was often short-tempered, had no time for fools, and could be merciless with anyone who crossed his path. At the same time we learn that he could also be caring, that he was protective of his pupils, and that he adopted two young men and helped them to good positions with those in power. Perhaps most surprisingly, we discover that he had an illegitimate child, a girl who tragically died in her infancy—an experience that must have marked him for life.

The aim of this series is to return to these earliest of records in order to unravel some of the legend and thereby recapture the real character of this enigmatic medieval swordsman. In following this rarely trodden trail the reader will soon find that the newly gained insights into Musashi's personality do not in the least diminish his stature but only serve to make him a more rounded character, a human being with whom we can all identify.

❷ The Origins of the Legend

The various sources collected here include those that were not necessarily written to extol the life and exploits of Musashi the swordsman. Instead, they are records in which Musashi makes his appearance because of his relation to the events described, or simply because of his relation to the author.

Thus the first cited record, the *Tomari jinja munefuda* is not so much a *denki*, but a record by Musashi's son celebrating the reconstruction of the Tomari shrine in his hometown of

Yoneda. Musashi is only mentioned because Iori happens to be his son. For the same reason, the *Hōkōsho* merely mentions Musashi because he happened to be the adoptive father of the author's uncle, Mikinosuke.

The opposite, of course, is true for the *Kokura hibun*, the epitaph to Musashi that can still be found on the memorial monument erected by Iori in Kokura a decade after his father had passed away. Among all the records of Musashi's exploits it is perhaps the most hagiographical.

Texts such as the *Yoshioka-den*, by contrast, were not so much written to extol Musashi's excellence in the art of swordsmanship, but rather that of his rivals. It should not surprise us, therefore, that the *Yoshioka-den*, the clan records of the Yoshioka clan, paint quite a different picture of Musashi's duels with their members, claiming that Musashi only fought two duels, failing to win the one and to show up for the other. Nor does the *Numata kaki* paint a very heroic picture of Musashi, claiming that it was his many *deshi* (students) who treacherously killed his opponent on Ganryū Island.

Luckily, the majority of texts take a more balanced approach. The *Honchō bugei shoden*, for instance, does not pronounce a clear winner in Musashi's duels with the Yoshioka clan, but achieves its unbiased stance by presenting different scenarios. And while it confirms that Musashi was victorious in his duel on Ganryū Island it is quick to recognize that his opponent "fought courageously with all his might, brandishing his sword with the speed of lightning." The *Kōkai fūhansō* has similar words of approval, painting him as "a tough man, who was very talented in the art of swordsmanship." It seems that, with the distance of time, the accounts gain in objectivity, for the *Gekken sōdan*, written more than one-and-a-half centuries after the events it describes, reserves equal space to describe the merits both of Musashi's school of swordsmanship and that of his opponent.

Other texts have yet different agendas. The *Tōsakushi* and the *Mimasaka ryakushi* specifically seek to connect Musashi to the province of Mimasaka, and in particular to Miyamoto village in the district of Yoshino. This would seem logical were it not that Musashi himself claims he was born in Harima, which had a village by the same name, making it possible for the *Harima kagami* to claim that Musashi instead "hailed from the village of Miyamoto in the vicinity of Ikaruga in the district of Ittō."

What all these texts do have in common is that they contribute their own specific insights into the man Musashi — the *Dōbō goen* on his relationship with women, the *Sieryūwa* on his qualities as a civil engineer, the *Kaijō monogatari* on his talents in the field of painting, and the *Bisan hōkan* on his mischievous sense of humor.

Though far from answering all our questions, these texts, which range from the early Edo period to the middle of the Meiji period, present us with a far fuller picture of Musashi — a man, after all, who led a largely wandering life and never entered the service of any lord, with the possible exception perhaps of Mizuno Katsunari, the feudal lord, or *daimyō*, under whom he took part on the siege of Osaka castle as a mounted guard of Katsunari's son and heir, an episode recorded in such glorious detail in the *Kōkō zatsuroku*.

❧ A Note on Dates and Names

All of these texts record events according to the Japanese, lunisolar calendar. Adapted from the Chinese system of keeping time, the calendar was based on the moon's cycle of 29.5 days with months assigned either twenty-nine or thirty days. This, however, caused a discrepancy between the calendar months and the seasons, so that, every few years, an additional month (*uruzuki*) was inserted to produce years with thirteen months. It is made all the more complex by the Japanese tradition of beginning a new Era (*nengō*) following the death of an emperor, a major calamity, or an auspicious event. This method of keeping time can lead to some confusion, particularly among Western readers, as the Japanese day, date, and year all fail to correspond to the Gregorian calendar. Thus, going by the lunisolar calendar, the *Kokura hibun* records that Musashi died on May 19 in the second year of Shōhō. According to the Gregorian calendar, however, the swordsman passed away on June 13, 1645. For historical interest, here, the original dating has been preserved, but to aid the modern reader Western dates have been added in brackets throughout the text.

When considering dates it is also important to take into account the traditional East Asian method of expressing age. Called *kazoedoshi* in Japan, this system dictates that newborns start life already at the age of one. Furthermore, each passing of a Lunar New Year, rather than the passing of one's birthday, adds a year to one's age. Given this way of counting, it might happen that people are up to two years older under the *kazoedoshi* system, when compared to the Western method of counting. Thus, when the *Kokura hibun* states that Musashi was thirteen years old when he fought his first duel, he was in fact not more than twelve years old by our reckoning. Similarly, he was only eight years old when he left his father to seek out his stepmother in Hirafuku.

Names are one of the least consistent factors in medieval Japanese texts. Birth, coming of age, succession, profession, high office, retirement, and death all had to find their expression in a person's name, and there are few, if any, persons of any significance in medieval Japan who went through life under one single name.

Musashi himself is a case in point. At the head of the *Kokura hibun* Iori introduces his father as Shinmen Musashi Genshin. In this he closely follows his adoptive father's example, for in his prologue to the *Gorin no sho* Musashi introduces himself as Shinmen Musashi no Kami Fujiwara no Genshin. It is clear why Musashi did so. Shinmen, the clan into which his father had married, was an ancient breed of warriors who had been involved in Emperor Godaigo's (1288–1339) failed attempt to restore power to the throne. That involvement led to exile, an exile from which they were eventually allowed to return and resume their role under the name of Shinmen, or "newly absolved."

Less easy to explain is Musashi's claim to Fujiwara descent. The Fujiwara had ruled the realm by proxy throughout the Heian period. As such they had successfully kept in check the two great military clans, the Taira and the Minamoto, and helped maintain the effeminate world of the court nobility. Nevertheless, there would have been few warriors in Musashi's day who would not have derived a great sense of pride in claiming some line of descent from such a powerful and illustrious clan, however tenable.

Finally, in the face of impending death, Musashi had to address another important aspect of his life as a warrior: how to assess his life's accomplishments and find peace with his own mortality. The *Kokura hibun*, the *Honchhō bugei shoden*, as well as the *Tōsakushi*, state that Musashi's Buddhist name was Niten, which tells us that Musashi was keen to be remembered for his Niten Ichi school of swordsmanship.

Japanese names in themselves are often difficult enough to distinguish from each other, let alone remember. So as not to further confuse matters, most characters in the text are identified by their common names, and not by their long titles of office or posthumous names.

Early Edo Texts
1653–96

The *Tomari Jinja munefuda* (1653)

The *Tomari Jinja munefuda* is the earliest extant record traceable to Musashi's adopted son Miyamoto Iori. Indeed, the *Tomari Jinja munefuda* also predates the *Kokura hibun* and as such is the first written record of Miyamoto Musashi.

The Tomari shrine was the family shrine of the Tawara clan. By the early seventeenth century the shrine had fallen into disrepair, but in the early fifties Iori and his relatives from Yoneda undertook to restore it. Work was completed in May 1653. To commemorate the occasion two *munefuda*s, narrow strips of thin wood stating the construction's donors, builder, and date of completion, were attached to the inner beams of the shrine's upper structure.

Hidden from public gaze, the *munefuda* carried their fortuitous message without being read, except perhaps by the occasional ignorant craftsman sent up for repairs, until 1916, when their texts were carried in full in the *Inami gunshi*, a collection of historical records collected and issued on behalf of the Inami district authorities.

It was not until 1960 that the two *munefuda* were "rediscovered" during a restoration of the roof of the shrine's *honden*, or sanctuary. It was only then, when the popularity of Musashi's story had reached its zenith, that their existence first received wide media attention and that their texts were carried and analyzed in numerous scholarly publications.

Ancestors

My ancestors are from the house of Akamatsu, descendants from Tomohira Shinnō, the seventh son of the sixty-second emperor,

Murakami. At the time of our distant ancestor Akamatsu Mochisada, an official at the Ministry of Justice, the clan fell on hard times. That is to say, being forced to shun the name of Akamatsu, they took on the name of Tawara and settled in the village of Yoneda, in the Kanan manor, in the district of Inami, in the province of Harima, where their children and their children's children were born.

My great grandfather was called Sadamitsu, my grandfather was called Iesada, and my father was called Hisamitsu. Through them, down to the present day, our family has served in the ranks of the Kodera. Indeed, even today their offspring live in the province of Chikuzen.

Among the Akamatsu diaspora of the province of Mimasaka were those who belonged to a line called the Shinmen. During the Tenshō era the Shinmen line came to an end at Akizuki castle in the province of Chikuzen because there was no successor. Heir to this house and heritage was a man named Musashi Genshin, who later took on the family name of Miyamoto. And since he did not have any children of his own, he adopted me as his son. Consequently, I still carry the family name of Miyamoto. During the Genna era (1615–24), at the time when I came of age, Ogasawara Tadazane, who hailed from the province of Shinano, took me in his service at Akashi, and I have remained so after he moved to Kokura.

❷ The Tomari Shrine

Through the name of "Tomari shrine" we honor the patron deity of the villages of Kimura, Kakogawa, Nishijuku, Funamoto,

Nishikawabara, Tomozawa, Ineya, Koshin, Jōshin, Yoneda (including Imazaike, Obata, Okuno, and Kitagawabara), Nakajima, Shio, and Ima, seventeen villages in all. According to that which is passed on by the town elders we are honoring the migration of the deity Hinokuma no Kami from Itō. Thus it is that Yonemura is also paying worship to the Kitano Tenmangu, which houses the spirit of Sugawara no Michizane.

As of late both shrines have sadly fallen into disrepair. My family and I lament this deeply. Thus it is that [through the shrine's restoration] in one way we offer our prayers for the prosperity of the house of Ogasawara, and in another way we seek to console the spirit of our ancestors.

My older brother, Tawara Yoshihisa, and my younger brothers, Ohara Genshō and Tawara Masahisa, among others, have seen to the completion of construction work so that now the shrine has acquired no less than two buildings. Such things are indispensable if the people are to receive from the heavens the favor of the gods. This is what is called "the true way of invoking the spirit." Thus it is that, even when we are not in prayer, we may know the benevolence of the gods. Yet while this is true it is in the nature of common people that their heavenly virtues are hidden. They cannot at first sincerely offer their true prayers simply at will. They should pray for good fortune and seek to realize their father's aspirations. And thus we pray that there may be mutual understanding between man and god.

The reason why my younger brother Genshō has become a member of the Ohara clan is that our mother was the only child of Ohara Nobutada, the successor to Ohara Nobutoshi, the master of Ohara castle in the Arima district of the province of Settsu. Having no sons of his own, Nobutada served in the ranks of Nakagawa Hidemasa and died in action in Korea. Hence, in accordance to our mother's wishes, Genshō took on and continued to carry the name of her father's clan.

Humbly recorded in the fifth month of second year of Shō-ō [May, 1653], Miyamoto Iori Sadatsugu.

- Tomohira Shinnō (964–1009) was an imperial prince of illustrious descent. Fathered by Emperor Murakami, his mother was Sōshi Nyo-ō, the second daughter of the great Daigō's third son, Yoshiaki Shinnō (904–37). Tomohira displayed a deep intellectual curiosity and fondness for learning. He grew up to become a gifted man of letters and a central figure at the court of Emperor Ichijō (980–1011), when the power of the Fujiwara regents was at its apex. Among his consorts at court were court ladies such as Sei Shōnagon and Murasaki Shikibu, who went on to become literary legends.
- Akamatsu Mochisada (13??–1427) was a great-grandson of the famed Akamatsu Norimura (1277–1350), who had helped found the Ashikaga shogunate and went on to become the *shugo* (governor) of Harima. Norimura's descendants continued to play an important role in the Ashikaga shogunate.

At Mochisada's time, Harima was governed by his second cousin, Mitsusuke. Yet it was Mochisada who was the favorite of shogun Ashikaga Yoshimochi (1386–1428) — so much so, that Yoshimochi (who was believed to be in a homosexual relation with his favorite), decided to deprive Mitsusuke of his lands and bestow them on Mochisada.

Enraged, Mitsusuke set fire to his mansion in the capital and withdrew to Harima, where he prepared for a final confrontation. In response, Yoshimochi ordered an army to be sent into Harima to punish the rebel, but the generals who had been summoned dallied and little happened.

The standoff was finally diffused when Bakufu officials (possibly having caught wind of the affair) appealed to Yoshimochi that Mochisada was to blame and Mitsusuke should be reinstated. Thus it was that Mochisada was forced to commit ritual suicide and Mitsusuke resumed his rightful position of governor of Harima.

- Sugawara no Michizane (845–903) was a famed poet-scholar who held important posts at the Heian court, but whose life took a tragic turn when he was unjustly accused of trying to usurp the power of the emperor and exiled to Kyushu. Pertinent here is that Iori's father had been a great admirer of Sugawara no Michizane. During his stay at the Tōkōin, in Nagoya, Musashi had composed a calligraphy with the text *namu Tenman Daijizai Tenjin*, a name used in reverence to the Heian court official.
- There is good reason why Iori should mention his younger brother. Genshō, after all, was a man of considerable standing. Having studied medicine in Kyoto he went on to become a high-ranking physician to the imperial household. Being bright and studious in nature the two brothers felt a close connection throughout their lives and, though Iori was buried in Kokura close to the monument to his father, a tombstone carrying the names of both brothers can still be found in the grounds of the Hōtō temple in Kyoto.

The *Kokura hibun* (1654)

The *Kokura hibun*, though not the oldest record of the life of Miyamoto Musashi, is one that occupies a special niche among the early records on Musashi. A lengthy epitaph celebrating the swordsman's life, exploits, and character, it is inscribed on a fifteen-foot obelisk-like stone memorial.

The monument was erected in 1654 on the initiative of Musashi's adopted son Miyamoto Iori, nine years after Musashi passed away. It stands on the crest of Temukeyama, a hill some two hundred feet in height on the outskirts of Akazaka, situated in the northern district of the port of Kokura. At the time of its erection the monument lay within Iori's fief in the district of Kikunokōri within the Kokura fiefdom in Buzen.

In 1887 the area underwent reconstruction to accommodate a gun battery guarding the Strait of Shimonoseki over which it looks. The monument was transferred to the nearby Enmeijiyama (Akazaka), while Iori's grave was moved to the southern foot of Temukeyama, close to the entrance of what is now called Temukeyama park. Since then Musashi's monument has been returned to its rightful place, at the top of Temukeyama, but the graves of Iori and his descendants remain at the foot of the hill.

The *Kokura hibun* is believed to have been written by Akiyama Wanao (1618–73), second abbot of the Taishō temple in Kumamoto. During Musashi's last years in Kumamoto, Wanao had befriended the swordsman and, according to the *Bukōden*, helped him in proofreading his *Gorin no sho*. He gave the swordsman his last rites, as well as his posthumous name.

In 1654, ten years after Musashi's death, Wanao is believed to have composed the lengthy epitaph in response to a request by Musashi's son.

> Looking up at the Heavens the True and Perfect Art of Heihō is Eternal, Even in Death.
>
> Heihōsha Without Equal under the Heavens
>
> Epitaph of Shinmen Musashi Genshin,
> last descendant of the Akamatsu of Harima.
> Died at Kumamoto in the province of Higo
> on May 19 in the second year of Shōhō [June, 13, 1645].
> Reverently erected on April 19,
> in the third year of Shōō [June 4, 1654]
> by his pious son.

❂ Musashi as a Man

"Look for the chances and respond to the changes," is the way of an accomplished general. The practice of the martial arts and the study of soldiery are the preoccupation of an army. Who was it that let his heart play at the gate of *bun* and *bu*, that let his hands work on the practice grounds of the martial arts, and gained fame for his courage in doing so? It was the noblyborn Musashi Shingen, scion of the Shinmen, last descendant of the Akamatsu of Harima, the man whose Buddhist name is Niten.

By nature he had a magnanimity of heart that did not care about trifles. Truly, was this not the man called Musashi Shingen?

❦ Early Years

He became the progenitor of the Niten art of *heihō*. The Buddhist name of his father, Shinmen, who came from a house known for its mastery of the *jitte*, was Muni. This tradition was passed on to Musashi, who, as a result of training from dusk till dawn, came to understand that the *jitte* was many times more efficient than a single sword. However, the *jitte* was not a conventional weapon, whereas it was normal for samurai to wear two swords. And since there was no harm in applying the principles of the *jitte* to the art of fighting with two swords, he chose to abandon the tradition of fighting with the *jitte* and founded one in which one fought with two swords.

Musashi truly was a rare swordsman. Whether he wielded a *shinken* or a *bokutō*, none could escape him, either by ducking or by running away. The force of his thrust was such that it resembled a projectile from a crossbow, and even the great Yōyū would not have been able to surpass him.

All things considered, Musashi was a man who totally mastered the art of *heihō* and embodied valor. Thus, at the age of twelve, he challenged to a duel a man by the name of Arima Kihei, a Shintō-ryū swordsman from Harima, and defeated him instantly. Then, in the summer of his sixteenth year, he went to the province of Tajima. There he again challenged a swordsman and struck him dead in the blink of an eye so that before long his name was known throughout town.

❂ The Yoshioka Clan

Afterwards, Musashi went up to Kyoto, where lived the Yoshioka, know as The Foremost Heihōsha in Japan. Musashi challenged them, and fought for his honor with a Yoshioka descendant by the name of Seijūrō on the grounds of the Rendai temple outside the old capital. It was supposed to be a real contest but Musashi floored Seijūrō with a single blow of his *bokutō*, causing the latter to pass out. And because it was agreed beforehand that they would only exchange a single blow, Musashi did not take Seijūrō's life. The latter's deshi came to his aid, lifted him on a stretcher, and took him home. There he was given various medical treatments and eventually recovered. In the end, he abandoned the martial life and took the tonsure.

However, Yoshioka Denshichirō, too, left Kyoto to fight it out with Musashi. He attacked Musashi with a five-foot-long *bokutō*. Seizing the opportunity, Musashi wrested the *bokutō* from him and struck him with his own weapon, so that Denshichirō fell to the ground and expired.

The followers of the Yoshioka school were filled with bitterness, conspiring among themselves saying "We cannot stand up to him with technical skill alone. Let us therefore resort to tactics." And thus, feigning that they had come to practice, Yoshioka Matashichirō and his deshi gathered and awaited Musashi in ambush outside Kyoto at Kudarimatsu.

There were several hundreds of deshi, intending to kill Musashi in a single attack with weapons, including bows and arrows. Musashi, however, had a talent for anticipating such events and, seeing through their dishonest scheme, he secretly said to his deshi: "This is no affair of yours. You must quickly leave this place. Even if my sworn enemies assembled an army, to me it would be no more than a drifting cloud, so why should I fear them?" And when Musashi proceeded to scatter his enemies apart it seemed as if a wild dog was chasing away wild beasts.

When Musashi returned to the capital having displayed his power, all its citizens were in awe. His gallant vigor, his superior calculation, defeating a vast force singlehandedly, these were the marvelous exploits of a man of war.

Now prior to this, successive generations of the Yoshioka clan had served as fencing instructors to the shogun. They were called "The Foremost Heihōsha in Japan." In the time of Shogun Yoshiaki, Musashi's father, Shinmen Munisai, was summoned to the capital and ordered to duel with the Yoshioka. Of the three bouts the Yoshioka swordsman won once, while Munisai won twice. In reward for this he received the title of "Heihōsha Without Equal in Japan." Given this precedent, when Musashi came to Kyoto and defeated the Yoshioka swordsmen several times, the Yoshioka school of swordsmanship ceased to exist.

❷ The Duel on Ganryū Island

Now near here there lived a master swordsman whose name was Ganryū. When Musashi made it known that he wanted to duel with Ganryū the latter proposed that they fight with real swords. But Musashi responded saying: "Feel free to use a real sword and display your skills with it, but I will fight with the *bokutō* and reveal its secrets." And thus both men solemnly pledged in writing that they would meet in duel on Funashima, an island in the sea between the provinces of Buzen and Nagato.

And it was on the island of Funashima that both men met at the same time. Ganryū came charging toward Musashi wielding his three-foot longsword, throwing at him all the techniques he had to his disposal. But Musashi struck him dead with one single blow of his *bokutō*, and with such speed that it seemed faster than lightning. Since Ganryū died on this island the people henceforth referred to it as Ganryū Island.

From his twelfth year until his prime of life Musashi fought more than sixty duels without ever being beaten. He would invariably say that "In order to seize victory, one has to strike one's opponent the very moment they raise their eyebrows in surprise." And each time he met with someone in duel he lived up to this dictum. From of old, thousands—nay tens of thousands—have met in duel. However, except for Musashi, I have never heard of anyone to squarely face a great swordsmen and strike him dead, be it in the present or the past, in the capital or in the countryside. By now Musashi's reputation has spread throughout the country and such is the extent of his undiminished fame that it is impressed on the minds of present-day people though the oral traditions of their elders. Truly, is it not a marvel, is it not a mystery? Indeed, the excellence of his precocious talent is unparalleled.

Musashi would often say that the art of *heihō* should mature in one's hands and govern one's heart, and that as long as one remains utterly unselfish and impartial one can command armies in the field and even the management of the affairs of state need not be difficult. Musashi's valor at the time of the rebellion started by Lord Ishida Mitsunari, the favorite of Taikō Toyotomi Hideyoshi, or at the time of the disturbance caused by Lord Toyotomi Hideyori, cannot be expressed in words, had oceans mouths or valleys tongues, and thus I will remain silent on the matter.

Not only was Musashi a consummate swordsman, he was also at home with etiquette, music, archery, horsemanship, calligraphy, arithmetic, and poetry. Moreover, be it in his dabbling in the arts or his skillful pursuit of his profession, he was never idle. He was the model of a fine human being.

Musashi died in the province of Higo. On his deathbed he wrote the words "looking up at the heavens the true and perfect art of *heihō* is eternal, even in death," and it was these words that have inspired me to commemorate his legacy. Hence, I, his pious son, have founded this monument, so that they may be passed on and seen by successive generations into eternity.

- Oddly, by stating that both swordsmen "met at the same time," Wanao seems to suggest that both swordsmen arrived at Ganryū Island (Funashima) at the same moment. Both the *Bukōden* and the *Bushū denraiki* claim that the men arrived at different times, although they fail to agree on who arrived first.
- It is typical, too, that Wanao has nothing to say about his hero's activities at the time of the Battle of Sekigahara and the sieges of Osaka castle, fourteen years later. It is perhaps rather due to his poor knowledge of Musashi's early life rather than his lack of words that the abbot—who was, after all, thirty-four years Musashi's junior—wisely chooses to remain silent on the issue.

🏵 The *Sōkyū-sama o-degatari* ^(165?)

The *Sōkyū-sama o-degatari* was written by Oba Heizaemon Toshiyuki, another close retainer of Mizuno Katsunari (1564–1651). Though the *Sōkyū-sama o-degatari* carries no date, Toshiyuki wrote his work probably sometime during the middle of the seventeenth century, for Sōkyū-sama, or master Sōkyū, is the Buddhist name of none other than his master Mizuno Katsunari. In his late seventies Katsunari had passed on the reins of his estate to his son and taken the tonsure. Though, like so many other retired warlords, he kept a close eye on the management of his fief, it seems he was serious about his religious commitments too. Thus, in 1643, at the respectable age of eighty, he spent a year in Kyoto's Daitokuji, at the end of which he received his Buddhist name of Sōkyū.

The fragment in which Musashi makes his appearance occurs in the course of the account of Mizuno Katsunari's prominent role in the suppression of the Shimabara Rebellion. With some six thousand troops, Katsunari's was the largest contingent contributed by a daimyo not from Kyushu. The excerpt describes the setting, on February 24, when Katsunari, now seventy-three, arrived in Shimabara and immediately convened a war counsel with the other commanders.

🏵 Mizuno Katsunari's Arrival at Shimabara

Having arrived at nightfall it was still pouring rain relentlessly when Lord Katsunari took control and ordered his troops in formation. Now, when the troops of the house of Ogasawara, who were in the vanguard, heard the inordinate clamor from the camp, they could tell that there might well be a method to this way of arriving and that it spoke of just how good a general Lord Katsunari was at that time.

Yet some began to talk among themselves and wonder how it could be that if there were, for instance, a sudden night attack such numbers would be of any use. Hearing this, a man by the name of Miyamoto Musashi said that he had ridden into battle under Lord Katsunari some years ago and that he was well acquainted with his manner of dispersing the troops, that he was a commander who exceeded the thought of commoners, and that his style of leadership was beyond reproach.

- Born at Kariya castle, in the province of Mikawa, the strands of Mizuno Katsunari's (1564–1651) clan were closely intertwined with those of the Tokugawa (then still the Matsudaira), who had their headquarters in the nearby castle of Okazaki. His aunt was none other than Ieyasu's mother, making Katsunari Ieyasu's cousin. Katsunari made his career in the Tokugawa ranks and fought numerous battles under Ieyasu, including the famous battles at Komaki and Nagakute (1584), the only time Ieyasu and Hideyoshi ever confronted each other on the field of battle.

  It seems that the young Katsunari was possessed of the same fierce temperament as Musashi, for it was during this battle that the young warrior landed himself in trouble when he killed one of his father's retainers in a fit of anger and he was expelled from Mikawa province for a while. It was partly through the intervention of his cousin, Ieyasu, that relations with his father were restored.

  Over the following years he continued to serve Ieyasu, most conspicuously so in the run-up to the Battle of Sekigahara, when he distinguished himself in the sieges of the castles of Gifu and Ōgaki. His loyalty gained him the rank of Fifth Level Retainer.

Exactly how Katsunari and Musashi first met is unclear, but it must have been their similarly fierce disposition that drew the two warriors together. Advanced in years and a man of high rank, Katsunari was very much Musashi's senior, but the great trust he put in the western warrior was revealed when he appointed Musashi as an attendant to his son Katsutoshi.

More proof of the close relation between Musashi and the house of Mizuno came shortly after, when Musashi, who had no sons of his own, adopted the third and fourth son of Nakagawa Shimanosuke, who served Katsunari as *musha bugyō*, the Magistrate of Warriors, during the siege of Osaka castle, a siege in which he lost his life. Shimanosuke hailed from the province of Ise, where he had been lord of Nakagawabara castle. Advanced in years, he had three sons, the two oldest of whom had taken part in the siege. They were old enough to vie for themselves, but the youngest, an eleven- year-old by the name of Mikinosuke, needed a guardian.

Another document that suggests a relationship between Musashi and Katsunari is a recently discovered copy of Musashi's *Heidō kagami* addressed to none other than Katsunari himself, though its provenance is disputed by some Japanese historians (see also the chapter on the *Gekken sōdan*). Today only copies of the *Heidō kagami* exist. Other extant copies, by contrast, only contain twenty-eight or even only twenty-one articles, but the copy addressed to Mizuno Katsunari consists of thirty-eight articles and ends with a postscript that runs as follows:

> Having collected in great detail the secret techniques for the correct transmission of my school of swords-

manship and calling it the *Heidō kagami*, I hereby grant this document as a license to my deshi to whom I have conveyed the full secrets of my art. I have recorded the unparalleled and unprecedented secrets of this art of *heihō* unrivaled in past and present, so that it may be preserved and perpetuated for eternity. No credence should be given to any license attributed to me if it does not include this secret scroll, even if it bears a signature in my hand. For how can one win a duel without studying the various tenets it contains?

Miyamoto Musashi no Kami Fujiwara Yoshitsugu
To master Mizuno Hyūga no Kami [Katsunari]

- The above document is one of the few surviving to carry the name Yoshitsugu. Another copy of the *Heidō kagami* (this time not addressed to Mizuno Katsunari) dated the eighth month of the eleventh year of Keichō (September 1606) carries the same name, as do a number of manuscripts related to Musashi's Enmei-ryū.

The quoted document is dated "an auspicious day," in the twelfth month of the thirteenth year of Keichō [January 1609]. This means that Musashi had met and befriended Katsunari by the time he was only twenty-five. This in itself makes sense, since at that age Musashi was still living in Edo developing his Enmei school of swordsmanship, while Katsunari would have frequented the new capital to visit his relatives at Edo castle.

It is more difficult to believe that, especially at this time in his life, when he had not yet fully established himself,

Musashi would have had the social standing to address such a document to a man of Katsunari's standing, regardless of their identical age. It is true, on the other hand, that Musashi had already made a name for himself by defeating the famed Yoshioka brothers (though this, in turn, is disputed by the *Yoshioka-den*), and it is not wholly unimaginable that Katsunari had somehow met and practiced with Musashi during his many visits to Edo.

This scenario also provides us with a clue as to how Musashi came to serve Katsunari during the siege of Osaka castle. If Katsunari had come to know Musashi in Edo and had been impressed with his skills, it is easier to understand that he would have chosen him to serve as his son's guard during such a dangerous campaign.

- The Shimabara Rebellion, so called after the peninsula on which it played out, was the last serious military conflict to upset the centrally imposed order of the Edo Bakufu. Chief source of the rebellion was the harsh regime of the local daimyo, Matsukura Katsuie (1598–1638), who imposed such heavy taxes on the already severely impoverished populace that many simply starved.

  The rebellion was led by a certain Amakusa Shiro, the son of a retainer of the Christian daimyo, Konishi Yukinaga. Shiro, too, was a Christian, and so were most of the rebels, who at the peak of the rebellion numbered more than twenty thousand. Among them were a considerable number of *rōnin*, masterless samurai, but most of them were simple peasants, who had been joined by their womenfolk and children and had ensconced themselves in Hara castle, which had been standing empty for several years.

  After the rebellion erupted on December 17, 1637, the first attempts to suppress it followed within weeks. They were undertaken by the governor of Nagasaki, but his forces, only a few thousand strong, suffered a crushing defeat and had to retreat to Nagasaki. The governor now called in the help of the Bakufu, and it was on their orders that the local military clans raised a force of well over a hundred thousand troops, including some six thousand raised by the Ogasawara.

Yet in spite of their overwhelming strength (and in spite of help from the Dutch, who fired more than four hundred rounds into the stronghold from one of their ships) it was not until April 15 before the stronghold finally fell to the Bakufu troops. More than ten thousand Bakufu troops died in the course of the siege, but all the rebels, including women and children were killed on the castle's fall.

The *Hayashi Razan bunshū* (1662)

Hayashi Razan (1583–1657) was a Neo-Confucian scholar who served as tutor the first four shoguns of the Tokugawa Bakufu. Razan was a man of demonic energy who almost single-handedly established Neo-Confucianism as the official Bakufu creed. He wrote countless scholarly works which were posthumously (1662) compiled into the *Hayashi Razan bunshū* (*The Collected Works of Hayashi Razan*) and the *Razan sensei isshū* (*Master Razan's Poems*) by his third son, Hayashi Gahō.

During his life, Razan amassed a vast library on the premise of his Edo residence, which he converted into a Confucian college called Kokunkan. It was Yamaga Sokō, incidentally, a student of that college, who took the first steps to codify the ethics of *bushidō*.

Tribute to Shinmen Genshin

"Hitting the whirlwind, hitting the row of racks," they are the falsehoods of Puhua. The green snake that leaps out of the inner sleeve, it is the magic of the mountain wizard. The swordsman Shinmen Genshin carries a sword in each hand and calls his school of swordsmanship the Nittō Ichi-ryū. Whether striking or stabbing, the modulation between right and left, the elasticity of right and wrong, are born in the mind and communicated to the hands, so that the strike becomes a crushing blow, the attack a crushing defeat, so that one is bound to say that "One sword cannot beat two." These are anything but the falsehoods of Puhua, the magic of the mountain wizard. How desirable it would be to have ten thousand of one's enemies study this art of *heihō*. For it is evocative of the long sword of the Marquis of Huaiyang, and with it the Chinese emperor would lose neither his right- nor his left-hand general. Truly, is such an art of *heihō* not worthy of being compared to the Chinese proverb that teaches us how one can conquer huge armies with small means?

- Puhua, or Fuke in Japanese, was a Chinese monk of the Tang dynasty and a student of the famous Linji Yixuan (800–866), founder of the Linji (Rinzai) School of Chan (Zen) Buddhism. Puhua is believed to have walked the streets carrying a large wind bell and chanting the kind of incantations Razan here quotes. Puhua's strand of Buddhism was introduced to Japan sometime during the thirteenth century, where it became known as Fuke Zen.
- The Marquis of Huaiyang, Han Xin (?–196 BC) was a Chinese military strategist who is believed to have studied the art of swordsmanship from his early youth. His martial genius led him to become a great military commander in the forces of Gaozu (256–195 BC), the first emperor of the Han Dynasty, the "Chinese emperor" to whom Razan is referring.

  Both the Marquis Han Xin and Emperor Gaozu feature prominently in the *Shiji*, the *Records of the Grand Historian*, one of the first systematic overviews of more than two thousand years of Chinese history, written between 109 and 91 BC by the famous Chinese historian Sima Qian (145–86 BC).

  The episode to which Razan refers concerns a critical stage in Gaozu's struggle against Qin dominance. It recounts how Han Xin, who was in charge of Gaozu's food stores, but aspiring to higher office, grows increasingly frustrated with general Xiao He, Gaozu's most trusted general, who has promised to introduce him to his lord. Then, during a lull in the fighting, Han Xin disappears. His disappearance coincides with the desertion of a large number of Gaozu's men, including Xiao He.

After two days Xiao He suddenly reappears. Asked by Gaozu to explain his conduct the general insists that he did not desert like the other men but had gone in pursuit of Han Xin, whom he has brought back. Surprised, Gaozu asks him why he did not go in pursuit of his other men, would that not have been a worthier cause? The general explains that Han Xin did not desert, that his strategic genius was invaluable, and that to lose both the marquis and himself would be tantamount to Gaozu losing both his hands. Swayed by this argument, Gaozu decides to appoint Han Xin as one of his generals.

The *Kaijō monogatari* (1666)

Completed in 1666, the *Kaijō monogatari* was written by a certain Sōan Echū (1628–1703), a by now largely forgotten monk from the Sōtō sect who began his monastic life in Kumamoto's Ryūchō monastery. Later in life he moved to Edo, where he became an acolyte of the more well-known Suzuki Shōsan (1579–1655), the author of works such as the *Inga monogatari* and the *Nenbutsu sōshi*.

Following his teacher's death in 1651, Echū traveled back to Kyushu, where he settled in Shimabara. It was there that he began to work on the *Kaijō monogatari*, which recounts the conversations between an old monk (supposedly Etchū himself) and his fellow travelers while crossing over from Nagasaki to Satsuma by boat in the summer of 1656. The work is cast in a question-answer form, in which complex Buddhist principles are explained in words and anecdotes that can easily be understood by commoners.

Given that Echū originally hailed from Kumamoto—where Musashi spent the latter part of his life—it is surprising that Echū does not dwell on Musashi's later life in Kyushu given the fact that he published his work more than two decades after the swordsman's death. Instead, the author simply states that Musashi "lived at Akashi in the province of Harima." Thus, the *Kaijō monogatari* merely deals with the swordsman's life during his stay at Akashi castle, and concentrates on Musashi's encounter with the rival swordsman Musō Gonnosuke Katsuyori, and his response to lord Ogasawara Tadazane (1596–1667), the daimyo of the Akashi fief (and later that of Kokura), who had asked him to paint an image of Dharma.

Moreover, that duel, though described in vivid detail, is the only such encounter mentioned in the *Kaijō monogatari*. This should not surprise us, for the author's real purpose is to make his point about the power of the Buddhist dharma. To do so he needed only one successful match with the sword to serve as a contrasting background against which he could then emphasize Musashi's hesitancy where it came to the creative art of painting—a hesitancy he could then attribute, not so much—as the swordsman himself explicitly states—to Musashi's deviation from the "martial Way" (*heihō*), but rather his deviation from the Buddhist Way (*butsuhō*).

Be that as it may, the mere fact that Musashi already appeared in such an early work attests to the fame he had already acquired among the populace within a decade of his death. That Etchū was able to make his particular point in reference to the swordsman's creative talents shows Musashi's art, too, had already left left a deep impression. It also suggests that besides teaching his art of swordsmanship and his work as a military advisor to Ogasawara Tadazane's construction magistrate, Musashi managed to dedicate a considerable amount of his time to writing calligraphy and creating *sumi-e*, or ink-wash paintings.

❷ The Duel with Musō Gonnosuke

There was a *heihōsha* by the name of Miyamoto Musashi. From the age of sixteen he dueled with many men of note, putting to his name as many as sixty duels, not one of them he failed to win. He lived in Akashi in the province of Harima.

One day a man visited Akashi, and asking for directions, he said: "I am Musō Gonnosuke. I hear that master Musashi is residing here and I have come to visit him." When Musashi's deshi came out to see who had come, they saw a stout man of six feet, armed with a longsword and in the company of eight deshi who seemed a match to any of themselves.

Now Gonnosuke was a famous man and Musashi's deshi, who had heard of his reputation, now saw themselves facing the man himself, as well as a large number of his followers, and not one of them did not feel his hair stand on end to some extent.

One of the two deshi who had gone out to greet them returned to Musashi and informed him of their arrival. Musashi, who was a crafting a toy bow from riverside willow, said "Tell them to come in." His deshi immediately invited Gonnosuke inside, but even when he came in and sat down this great man impressed them with his air of authority.

It was the month of August, yet in spite of the season he was wearing a double winged *haori*. Draped from his shoulder to his waist, he wore a crimson banner on which written in gold characters were the words "Musō Gonnosuke, first and foremost founder of the Japanese art of *heihō* under the heavens." His eight deshi, too, sat down in front of Musashi and seeing this Musashi's deshi realized this was a serious affair that might well get out of hand as they held their swords at the ready and anxiously observed the men in question.

Musashi, however, seemed utterly at ease as he continued to work on his toy bow and said: "So you are Gonnosuke. It is some time since I last heard your name but I have not had the opportunity of meeting you, and I am glad that you have come to visit me." Gonnosuke replied: "Indeed, it is as you say. I have long wanted to meet with you in duel, but was unable to do so thus far. I was on my way to Kyushu when the boat on which

I traveled called at Akashi, but when I heard that you were staying here I decided to visit you."

Turning the subject to the art of *heihō*, Gonnosuke said: "I am on a *musha shugyō*. Needless to say that I have visited the Kantō region and as far as the northern provinces, yet while I have engaged in a number of *shiai* I have not yet encountered my equal, so I made up my mind to visit the western provinces. I have seen you father Muni wield the *tachi*, but hear that now that his art has been passed on to you the use of the *tachi* has changed. Could you not give me a brief demonstration of the way in which it has changed?" But Musashi answered: "If you have seen my father's art of wielding the *tachi*, you will find that mine has not particularly changed at all."

But Gonnosuke politely insisted, saying: "Please, for the sake of my *deshi*, let us have a bout with the *tachi*."Then Musashi replied: "My art of *heihō* is not suitable to perform [the offensive role of] *uchidachi*, as it has been construed in such a manner that it will stop an opponent's sword in whatever way he responds. So if you agree we could have a bout in which you take on the role of *uchidachi*." Gonnosuke rejoiced, saying: "In that case, let me take on the role of *uchidachi*!" And while he said so, he produced from a silk cover a four-foot staff reinforced with steel from top to bottom.

Musashi, who was still holding the branch of riverside willow, stood up and said: "Well, feel free to strike." At this, Gonnosuke immediately charged with his staff, but each time he struck out Musashi stopped him with a few light parries of his piece of willow. Gonnosuke now changed the grip on his staff and struck out with a horizontal blow, touching the collar of Musashi's *haori* just below his sleeve. He cried out in a loud voice: "I struck you! I struck you!" But Musashi said: "No! One cannot call that a strike. What good would such a strike do? Let me show you what a real strike is."

Gonnosuke grew red in the face as he concentrated on an opening in Musashi's defense, but he failed to find one and suddenly found himself veering backward. Musashi had driven Gonnosuke into a corner of the room and had landed a fierce blow on his forehead, which immediately swelled red. Gonnosuke acknowledged defeat and, regretting his folly, became Musashi's deshi.

- A *tachi* is the longest of the pair of swords traditionally worn by samurai.
- *Uchidachi*, or "striking *tachi*," is used to describe the offensive role in practicing a fencing technique. The *uchidachi*, which is usually performed by the senior sparring partner, takes the initiative by making the first move, thus allowing the *shidachi*, or "receiving *tachi*," to respond and practice a specific technique by striking the winning blow. What Musashi is saying, then, is that in his art of fencing the opponent is never able to strike a blow, let alone a winning one.

❧ A Special Request

Since Musashi also was an adept in the art of the brush, one day his lordship requested that he should do a painting of Dharma. That is, he should do a painting in the presence of his lordship. Yet Musashi could not bring himself to paint well, and each time he tried the result was worse. He painted with all his might, but somehow it would not come out the way he wanted. In the end, after a day of trying in vain, he decided to go to sleep.

That night he suddenly rose from his bed and said: "The reason why I wasn't able to paint well was because I failed to apply the art of *heihō* in which I excel." Ordering his deshi to make light he began painting. And lo and behold the result was staggering.

When afterwards his deshi questioned him and asked why it was that he was suddenly able to paint he answered and said: "I was unable to paint well because I had forgotten about the art of *heihō* and thus became hesitant in the presence of his lordship. Whenever I pass on the art of *heihō* and take up the *tachi*, I forget myself and those around me and it is as if heaven and earth erupt. What are high rank or low birth to me? It is because I adhered to this principle that the painting turned out well." Hearing this his deshi were deeply impressed.

Like the old masters who taught that "When practitioners of the martial way take up their *tachi* they achieve a detached state of mind, yet as soon as they put their *tachi* down again they become ordinary persons. Practitioners of the Buddhist way, however, are not only always in a state of transcendence, no matter what situation they encounter, they do not lose the power of the Buddhist dharma, but can apply it at will." It was these teachings that Musashi spoke of. Thus it was that Musashi was able to use the power of the Buddhist dharma when practicing the martial way, yet became hesitant when he was required to draw a painting.

- Dharma, in Buddhism, refers to the cosmic law and order although it is also frequently used in reference to Buddha himself or his teachings.

❂ The *Numata kaki* ⁽¹⁶⁷²⁾

The *Numata kaki*, the family records of the Numata clan, was compiled in 1672 by a descendant of Numata Nobumoto. Nobumoto was the keeper of Moji castle, situated some ten miles northwest of Kokura, and the castle where Musashi stayed at the time of his famous duel with Sasaki Kojirō on nearby Hikojima (also Funashima, or Ganryū Island).

Drawing largely on Nobumoto's written memoirs, the *Numata kaki* consists of two parts, the first being a largely chronological account of Nobumoto's life and times, written down in twenty-nine lengthy paragraphs. Though the *Numata kaki* does not dwell on the events on the island itself, it does offer a fascinating insight into the conflict that erupted among the followers of both swordsmen in the wake of the duel.

❂ The Duel on Hikojima Island

One year, at the time when master Nobumoto resided at Moji castle, Miyamoto Musashi Genshin visited Buzen and instructed his lordship in the Nitō school of swordsmanship. At that time, there was a man by the name of Kojirō who used the Ganryū method of combat, in which he too acted as instructor. The deshi of both men contested the superiority of their masters' styles of fencing, so it was decided that Musashi and Kojirō should engage in a *shiai*, which was to be held on the island of Hikojima (later called Ganryū Island) situated between the province of Buzen and Nagato. They decided that they would not bring along a single deshi, and when they finally met in duel Kojirō was killed.

Kojirō had not brought along any deshi, as agreed, but Musashi's deshi had come to the island and hidden themselves. Following the duel Kojirō regained consciousness, yet Musashi's deshi ganged up on him and killed him. Word of this got out to Kokura, where Kojirō's deshi formed a gang that crossed over to Funashima in large numbers hoping to slay Musashi. It was for this reason, in order to avoid trouble, that Musashi fled to Moji, seeking the help of master Nobumoto, who acquiesced and gave Musashi shelter at his castle, so that the latter was spared.

Afterward, Musashi was brought to the province of Bungo. He was given an escort by Ishii Mitsunojō, who secured the way with men on horseback armed with muskets, ensuring that Musashi arrived in Bungo unharmed. There he delivered him to the house of a man by the name of Munisai.

- Numata Nobumoto was a retainer of Hosokawa Tadatoshi (1586–1641) and the keeper of Moji castle. Following the castle's dismantlement in the wake of the Bakufu's one-castle-per-fief edict of 1616, Nobumoto moved to Kokura, where he died in 1624.
- Though the *Numata kaki* is not the only account to claim that Kojirō was killed by Musashi's deshi (see, for instance, the *Saiyū zakki*) one reason for this differing account may be that Nobumoto's descendant sought to emphasize Musashi's vulnerability in order to highlight his ancestor's importance in offering the swordsman a safe haven.

The *Yoshioka-den* (1684)

The *Yoshioka-den* (also *Yoshioka kaden*) is one of the few records to give us a perspective from one of Musashi's adversaries. The *Yoshioka-den* was written by Fukuzumi Dōyō. Born in 1625 in the province of Awa, Dōyū studied medicine under a man named Kinoshita Kyōrin and began practicing in Osaka in his early twenties.

Dōyū seemed to have been a competent physician, for many of his contemporaries studied medicine under him, yet his real interest lay in the field of history. From an early age he had been gathering old records, including genealogical tables, and war records. By the time he reached his fifties he was a well-known genealogist and biographer. It was probably more for his qualities as a chronicler than his medical expertise that, in 1684, at the age of 59, Dōyū entered the service of Matsudaira Yoritsune and was put in charge of the huge archive of the Takamatsu fiefdom.

Dōyū did not serve Yoshitsune for long. He died in 1689, after serving the daimyo for only five years. Yet it was probably during his five years in Takamatsu that the historian came into the possession of the family records (*kaden*) of the famous Yoshioka clan.

Issued in 1684, the *Yoshioka-den* remains one of the few sources on a school of swords that enjoyed such high status under the Ashikaga Bakufu. It is clear that Dōyū was a man of learning who was trained in the classical school, for the *Yoshioka-den* is written in *kanbun*, a method of annotating classical Chinese texts so that it could be read in Japanese.

- *Kanbun* was the writing style of intellectuals and of (Bakufu) officials, right up to the end of the Tokugawa period.

❂ The Yoshioka Tradition of Swordsmanship

The Yoshioka brothers from Kyoto were famed for their school of swordsmanship—a school unprecedented in past or present for its technical skill. The older brother was called Genzaemon Naotsuna, the younger brother was called Mataichi Naoshige, but they were better known as the Kenpō Brothers.

Their art of swordsmanship derived from the school practiced by Genbō Hideyuki, as well as the old Satō, Suzuki, and Soga traditions. The members of house of Yoshioka were a sincere people, with a good sense of tradition and keen to uphold the law, for which reason the common people referred to their patriarch as Kenpō, or Justice. Their great-grandfather was called Naomoto, an official at shogunal court of Ashikaga Yoshiharu, and a man of martial accomplishments. Their grandfather, Naomitsu, as well as their father, Naokata, were accomplished masters of their art. Yet it was under the two brothers [Naotsuna and Naoshige] that the Yoshioka-ryū prospered with each new day and that it surpassed the art practiced by previous generations.

For this reason there was such a large number of swordsmen who studied under their tutelage that it was impossible to count them all. Now among the swordsmen throughout the country there were only four of five with the skill to challenge them—men such as Asayama Santoku who hailed from Shikoku and Kyushu, Kashima Rinsai, a practitioner of the Shintō-ryū who hailed from the Kantō region, and a certain Miyamoto Musashi, a swordsman famous in northern Echigo, Mutsu, and Dewa for a style of swordsmanship called Muteki-ryū.

- Yoshioka Genzaemon Naotsuna was the eldest son of Yoshioka Naokata, *shihan* to the then shogun Ashikaga Yoshiaki (1537–97), and the man who had dueled with Musashi's father.
  The *Yoshioka-den* is the only record to pit Naotsuna against Musashi in duel. Thus the *Koro usawa* speaks of a Yoshioka Kanefusa, while the *Gekken sōdan* mentions a Yoshioka Kenpō, a name usually associated with the school's founder, Yoshioka Naomoto. The *Kokura hibun*, the *Bushū denraiki* and the *Bukōden* all claim that the first Yoshioka member to confront Musashi in duel was a man by the (middle) name of Sejūrō. Given that this was merely his common name, it is still possible that Seijūrō and Naotsuna were one and the same person, i.e., Yoshioka Seijūrō Naotsuna. However, this would be to ignore the fact that there are no records to mention this name in full and that the *Yoshioka-den* claims the man's full name was Yoshioka Genzaemon Naotsuna and not Yoshioka Seijūrō Naotsuna.
- Yoshioka Mataichi Naoshige was Naokata's second son. The same controversy that surrounds Naotsuna as Musashi's first opponent surrounds Naoshige as his second. Again the *Kokura hibun*, the *Bushū denraiki* and the *Bukōden* all claim that Musashi's second opponent was a man by the name Yoshioka Denshichirō. The *Yoshioka-den* is the only record to mention Naoshige's name in this connection.
- Yoshioka Naomoto was a merchant of dyed goods who had been trained in the Kyohachi school of fencing. Naomoto developed his own style of fencing, called the Yoshioka-ryū, and became the private fencing instructor to the twelfth Ashikaga shogun, Yoshiharu (1511–50).

- Yoshioka Naomitsu. The success of the Yoshioka clan reached its zenith under Kenpō's younger brother, Naomitsu, who established the Heihōsho, a martial arts school in the capital's Imadegada district.

◉ The Duel with Miyamoto Musashi

Miyamoto Musashi was a retainer of general [Matsudaira] Tadanao from Echizen and a master in the art of fighting with two swords. Tadanao practiced the art of swordsmanship under Musashi and there was not a moment that Musashi was not by his side.

One day, when Tadanao was at the Jūrakudai, he spoke to Musashi and said: "The Yoshioka brothers are famous and have won countless *shiai*. They are true masters of their craft. What if we were to pit the Yoshioka against you in a bout?" Musashi humbly answered: "Even if both brothers came at me at once, they would not stand a chance, even against a single sword of mine." At this Tadanao rejoiced and sent word of their intent to Kyoto's shoshidai Itakura Iga no Kami Katsushige. Itakura Katsushige immediately summoned the two Yoshioka brothers and said to them: "It seems that the Miyamoto clan wants to match their skill with you in a bout. Quickly decide your course of action and submit your plans to his lordship's inspection." The two brothers reverently accepted the challenge.

Yoshioka Genzaemon Naotsuna was the first to step forward and match his skill with Musashi. Both men exerted their mental powers against each other, but already shortly into the bout Musashi was struck on the forehead and lost a lot of blood.

When Naotsuna stepped back the crowd cried out that it had been Naotsuna's victory. Yet others said that it was a draw. Angered, Naotsuna said: "In that case, let us have another contest to make clear who is the winner." At this Musashi said: "My contest with Naotsuna is done. Now I want to fight with Mataichi Naoshige."

Thus a day was chosen which the two men would fight each other and everyone waited in anticipation for the contest. However, when the day finally came Musashi had disappeared and no one knew where he had gone. Thus it was that the people said that Naoshige had won the contest sitting down.

- While this is one of the few text to have been written in support of the Yoshioka clan there a several problems concerning its veracity. The first dissonant is Dōyū's claim that Musashi was a swordsman known in the provinces of Echigo, Mutsu, and Dewa, all provinces situated in the northern regions of Japan's main island of Honshu. No mention is made of Musashi's roots in Harima, or his protracted stay on the island of Kyushu.

  A second point is Dōyū's claim that Musashi was a retainer of Matsudaira Tadanao (1595–1650), daimyo of the Fukui fief in Echizen. There are no other sources that support the idea that Musahi ever entered anyone's service, let alone that of a daimyo with a fief on the northwest coast of Japan where he had no roots. Indeed, the *Yoshioka-den* is the only record to link Musashi to Japan's northern provinces. If Dōyū claim is true, it would mean that lord Tadanao was only ten at the time of Musashi's encounter with the Yoshioka brothers. Moreover, Tadanao only came of age and succeeded his father, Yūki Hideyasu (1574–1607), in

1607. While it is not impossible that Tadanao was present at the bout, there are no other sources that support this view.

A far more likely contender, for instance, would be Matsudaira Katsutaka (1589–1666), the man whom Musashi visited in 1633 when he left Nagoya to rejoin his son in Kokura (see the *Bushū denraiki*.) Only a few years younger than Musashi, Katsutaka was distantly related to the Ogasawara and known to be a fervent aficionado of the martial arts. He was also an important Bakufu official and therefore likely to regularly visit the Kyoto. If it was indeed Katsukata who arranged Musashi's famous *shiai* with the Yoshioka brothers, it is not surprising that Musashi was eager to visit the Bakufu official on his way to Kokura.

Another discrepancy is the suggestion that Tadanao stayed at the famous Jūrakudai. Completed in 1587, the Jūrakudai was Toyotomi Hideyoshi's lavish official residence from 1588 onwards and remained so until 1591, when Hideyoshi resigned his post as *kanpaku*. That position was assumed by his nephew Hidetsugu, but when, in 1595, the latter was forced to commit *seppuku*, the Jūrakudai was dismantled, although some of its buildings have survived to this day.

☯ The *Hōkōsho* (1696)

The *Hōkōsho* was drawn up in 1696, and submitted to the administrators of the Okayama fiefdom in the province of Bizen by a certain Miyamoto Kōhei, a nephew of Mikinosuke and head of a contingent of *ashigaru* of Ikeda Masakoto (1645–1700), the second son of the master of Okayama castle, on a stipend of two-hundred-and-fifty *koku*. Kōhei was fifty-five at the time, which means that, though he never knew Mikinosuke, he might have known Musashi's other adopted son, Iori, who would have visited the neighboring province of Harima regularly during the reconstruction of the Tomari shrine (see the chapter *Tomari jinja munefuda*).

If we are to believe the *Hōkōsho*, Mikinosuke had a younger brother by the name of Kurōtarō, who was living with him at the time he served Honda Tadatoki (1569–1626). This would suggest that Musashi not only adopted Mikinosuke after the siege of Osaka castle, but also his younger brother. No other record, however, makes any mention of Kurōtarō, and it is possible that Mikinosuke took his younger brother under his wings on his own account, after he entered Tadatoki's service sometime after 1617 (the year in which Tadatoki was promoted to his new fief of Nitta in Harima).

Kurōtarō succeeded his brother after the latter followed his master in death in 1626 at the age of twenty-three. Following Tadatoki's death, Kurōtarō accompanied his wife, Senhime and her daughter, Katsuhime, on their visit to Edo under the *sankin kōtai* system. Katsuhime later married Ikeda Mitsumasa (1609–82), which is how Kohei came to be a retainer of the Ikeda clan, for he was Kurōtarō's second son.

Our ancestors hailed from a small castle in a place called Nakagawabara. My grandfather was Nakagawa Shimanosuke, who in his youth led a wandering life, until he entered the service of Lord Sengoku Gonbei [Hidehisa], who at that time had his seat of power in the province of Sanuki. Having served his lord in battle with valor countless times, he became a leader of a unit of riflemen on a stipend of some one thousand *koku*.

At one stage, in reward for outstanding service, he was granted the honor of including in his own family crest the first character, *ei*, for "eternal," of Lord Gonbei's family crest of *eiraku*, or "eternal bliss." At this time Lord Mizuno Hyūga no Kami [Katsunari], who was still called Rokuzaemon, fell out of favor with his father, Izumi no Kami, and also joined master Gonbei. From that moment onward they became friends, so that even after they had parted they sought each other's friendship, due to which, afterwards, Lord Hyūga no Kami spoke to my grandfather, asking him to join him. Thus it was that my grandfather entered the service of Lord Mizuno Hyūga no Kami as a Magistrate of Warriors on a stipend of six hundred *koku* and received the name Hanagami.

Now my so-called adoptive "grandfather," Miyamoto Mikinosuke, was Nakagawa Shimanosuke's son, and thus in reality my uncle. He was the adopted child of a man who called himself Miyamoto Musashi and entered the service of master Honda Tadatoki as a page when still young on a stipend of seven hundred *koku*. As one of his servants, he was allowed to wear Tadatoki's family crest of the Nine Whirlwinds, which was his lordship's alternative family crest. His lordship passed away on the seventh day, in the fifth month of the third year of Kanei [June 30, 1626], and on the thirteenth day of the same month [July 7, 1626], at the age of twenty-three, Mikinosuke followed his master in death.

My father, Miyamoto Kurōtarō, lived together with Mikinosuke and served Lord Tadatoki as a page. When Mikinosuke followed his master to the grave, Kurōtarō, since there was no one to succeed Mikinosuke, entered the service of his Lordship Honda Tadamasa and likewise took on the name of Mikinosuke. And when Tadatoki's widow, Senhime, traveled up to Edo from Harima, my father accompanied her and his Lordship Tadamasa and was invited to an audience by Senhime and Lord Tadamasa while they stayed at an inn on the way there. And during the time of Lord Honda Masatomo, he became the captain of his lordship's page corps. At the time of Honda Masakatsu, Kurōtarō fell ill while serving in the fiefdom of Kōriyama in the province of Yamato and passed away in the ninth month of the nineteenth year of Kanei [Juni 1642].

When Kurōtarō passed away, my brother, Bennosuke, became the head of the family and served Lord Masakatsu until the latter passed away when Bennōsuke was still young, causing him to be reduced to a *rōnin*.

I was born in the Kōriyama fiefdom in the province of Yamato and lost my brother, Bennosuke, at the age of fifteen. From that time onward I lived in Nara until, on the twelfth day of the tenth month of the second year of Kanbun [November 22, 1662] I was called in front by my current lord [Ikeda Masakoto] in Kōfu [in Mimasaka province] and entered his service on the tenth day of the eleventh month [December 20, 1662]. At present I have a stipend of sixty-two *koku* and have at my disposal five servants, and serve my master as attendant and messenger.

- Sengoku Hidehisa (1552–1614) was the head of the Komoro fief in the province of Shinano.
- Honda Masatomo (1599–1638) was Honda Tadamasa's second son and (due to the premature death of Tadatoki) became the second daimyo of the Himeji fief.
- Honda Masakatsu (1614–1671) was the oldest son of Honda Masatomo and the third daimyo of the Himeji fief until, in 1638, he was transferred to the fief of Kōriyama in Yamato province.
- The *Tōsakushi* is the only other record to suggest Musashi might have had another adopted son. Confusingly, it claims that the boy was called Shume and that he "was in the service of the Lord of Kokura, from the house of Ogasawara, and became a chief retainer with a fief of three thousand *koku*." Obviously, its author, Masaki Teruo, who served Matsudaira Yasuchika, the daimyo of the Tsuyama fief in Mimasaka, is confusing things. It was, of course, Iori who served Ogasawara Tadazane and moved with him to Kyushu when the latter was promoted to the Kokura fief.
- Interestingly, while Kurōtarō is often referred to as Musashi's third adopted son, technically, he would have been Musashi's second adopted son, making Iori Musashi's third adopted son. Kurōtarō, after all, had been orphaned along with his brother in 1615, when their father fell in the summer siege of Osaka castle. If Musashi indeed also took Kurōtarō under his wings following the siege, he would have done so several years before he adopted Iori.

Mid-Edo Texts
1704–90

The *Kōkai fūhansō* (1704)

The *Kōkai fūhansō* was written by Tachibana Shigetane, the father of Tachibana Minehira, author of the far more widely known *Bushū denraiki*. Shigetane was a chief retainer of Kuroda Mitsuyuki (1628–1707), the third generation daimyo of the Fukuoka fiefdom in the province of Chikuzen.

With a total revenue of five-hundred-and-twenty thousand *koku* the Fukuoka fiefdom was the seventh largest in the realm. As chief retainer to such an influential lord, Mitsuyuki occupied a position of great status and the size of his fief was commensurate. With a yield of ten thousand *koku*, it was large enough to support the same number of men for a year.

While Minehira's *Bushū denraiki* is now rightly known as one of the most authoritative medieval texts on Musashi, Shigetane's work has its own value, if only because it highlights the uncertainly around the identity of Musashi's opponent during his famous duel on Ganryū Island.

Yet it also provides its own details of interest, such as the long-standing enmity that existed between that very rival and Musashi's father, Muni—an enmity that may well have been the chief motive for Musashi to take part in the duel that was to play such an important role in establishing his reputation. It also claims that Musashi was not as confident of the outcome as some of the other accounts suggest.

Ganryū Island

The belief that Ganryū Island was named after a swordsman by that name is a mistake, for it was named after a school of swordsmanship. The founder of this school of fencing was a man by the name of Ueda Sōnyū. He spent a year in meditation on a rocky beach and, observing how the waves broke on the rocks below, devised a school of swordsmanship that he named Ganryū, or the "School of the Rocks."

A man by the name of Miyamoto Musashi lived here. His father was Miyamoto Munisai. They were natives of Chikuzen. When Musashi grew up he wandered around the country in the pursuit of *musha shugyō* and ended up in Kokura in the province of Buzen, where he stayed in the castle town of the Hosokawa clan. At this time Ueda Sōnyū stayed in the province of Nagato as an instructor in the Gan school of swordsmanship, and he criticized Musashi's art of combat. Given that his father, Muni no Suke, and Sōnyū held a grudge with respect to their art of combat, Musashi wanted to meet with Sōnyū in duel, so that they agreed to meet on the said island.

- Shigetane is the only biographer to mention the name Sōnyū. This is all the more remarkable when we consider that Shigetane's son, Minehira, the author of the far more widely known *Bushū denraiki*, did not follow his father's example, but instead referred to Musashi's opponent by the name Ganryū. In doing so, Minehira seems to have deliberately gone against his father, who specifically states that the island was named after the swordsman's Gan school and not after the swordsman (Ueda Sōnyū) himself.

🟤 The Duel

Musashi's attire on the day of duel consisted of a satin undergarment, which he wore as a jacket, and he was armed with a five-foot staff reinforced with metal. He crossed over to the island before Sōnyū, sat himself down and waited. Sōnyū wore a *dō-maru* suit of armor under his overcoat, and had a three-foot-one-inch long Aoe *tachi* inserted in his belt; he crossed over in a small boat, brandishing a *bokutō* in his hands.

One can only imagine what he thought when he saw that Musashi had crossed over before him. Drawing the Aoe sword he cut the sword's sheath in two and cast it into the sea. The *bokutō*, too, he threw into the sea as he came ashore and immediately went up to Musashi, brandishing his sword.

When Sōnyū lashed out toward the lining at the bottom of his kimono, Musashi leapt into the air and struck Sōnyū's head with his staff, causing him to fall. At this point the tip of Sōnyū's sword cut through the front of Musashi's *tadzuke hakama*, causing the garment to drop to his knees. Musashi did not move from where he was standing, and when Sōnyū tried to get up, he struck him down there and then.

Musashi then boarded a small boat and returned to Kokura. When Musashi tried to push the boat out to sea, one of the onlookers said, "Sōnyū, what happened? Bennosuke (which was Musashi's name at the time) is getting away." At this Sōnyū rose and yelled, "Bennosuke, where are you going?" upon which he dropped down dead.

It is true that Sōnyū lost in this duel, but he was a tough man, who was very talented in the art of swordsmanship. He also had many deshi in the western part of Honshu. They wanted to slay Musashi but it did not turn out that way.

- A *dō-maru* was one of three types of armor worn by medieval Japanese warriors. The *ō-yoroi*, or "large suit of armor," was the most elaborate suit of armor, and worn chiefly by the upper class of warriors, though it was designed with mounted archers in mind.

  Heavy, expensive, and difficult to wear, the box-shaped *ō-yoroi* gradually made way for the more comfortable *dō-maru*, or "around the body," or "body wrap," which was made of small scales of hard leather or metal laced into plates by means of cord and lacquered. To reduce the weight metal scales were only applied to those areas that protected the body's vital parts. Eight flexible skirt plates (*kusazuri*), as opposed to the *ō-yoroi*'s four, protected the lower body, while each shoulder was protected by a broad plate (*sode*). The throat was protected by a separate plate (*nodowa*).

  The *haramaki*, or "belly wrap," finally, was the simplest type of armor. Designed for *ashigaru*, it was originally made of the same materials as the *ō-yoroi*, but lacked a helmet (*kabuto*) and plates to protect the arms and legs. Over time the *haramaki* was gradually adopted by mounted warriors, causing it to evolve into a full-blown suit of armor alongside, yet with features distinct from, the *dō-maru*.

- Similar to his antagonists in earlier duels, not a lot is known about the man with whom Musashi set out to meet at Funashima. Most records fail to agree even on his name. The *Kokura hibun*, the lengthy epitaph found on the monument erected near Kokura in 1654 in Musashi's honor, merely mentions that the man is called Ganryū. The *Bushū denraiki* and its spin-off, the *Heihō senshi denki*, by contrast claim the man was named Tsuda Ganryū. The *Bukōden*, on the other hand, identifies Musashi's opponent as Ganryū Kojirō. So does its spin-off the *Nitenki*, although the latter also uses the name Sasaki Kojirō. The family name of

Sasaki occurs in a few other works that appeared during the eighteenth century, leading some to believe that his real name must indeed have been Sasaki Kojirō. There is, however, little evidence to support this claim, and the name may even have been an invention of the early eighteenth century Kabuki playwrights, who gave their villain such varying names as Sasaki Ganryū, Ganryū Kojirō, or Sasaki Kojirō.

If, as most sources have it, the name of the swordsman in question was indeed Sasaki Kojirō, Musashi was pitted against a representative of the Toda school of swordsmanship. Sasaki Kojirō is believed to have been a native of Echizen province, and born in the town of Fukui toward the middle of the sixteenth century. At a young age he entered the service of the powerful Asakura clan, which had its headquarters at Ichijōdani castle.

The Asakura were great patrons of the martial arts, especially of the Toda school of fencing, which traced its ancestry back through Chūjō Nagahide, all the way to the legendary fifteenth-century monk-warrior Nenami Jion and his Nen school of swordsmanship. Chief propagator of the Toda-ryū in Kojiro's days was the famous Toda Seigen, who had under his wing a large number of aspiring swordsmen, including his star deshi Yamazaki Rokusaemon (who was later adopted by the Toda and given the name Toda Shigemasa), and Kanemaki Jisai.

Under Jisai, Kojirō acquired many of the Toda techniques, among them the famous *tsubame-gaeshi*. Following the destruction of the Asakura clan by Oda Nobunaga's forces in 1570 he embarked on a *musha shugyō* under the spiritual name of Ganryū, until, somewhere around the turn of the seventeenth century, he became a fencing instructor to Hosokawa Tadaoki (1563–1646), the lord of Kokura castle in Buzen, the most northern province of Kyushu.

🌀 Aftermath

Afterwards, Musashi went to the Kyoto-Osaka region and stayed in Hyōgo for two years. After that he went to the province [sic] of Akashi and stayed as the guest of Ogasawara Tadazane.

Unable to forget the fervor with which Lord Hosokawa Tadatoshi pursued the art of *heihō*, Musashi again went down to the western provinces. By then Lord Hosokawa had become the lord of Higo, and thus Musashi went to Higo and stayed as Lord Hosokawa's guest and taught the art of *heihō*. At the time of the duel on Ganryū Island he was eighteen and not yet matured in the art of swordsmanship. Later, in old age, he would say that he had done it in the heat of youth, but that at the time, in his heart of hearts, it was not something he believed he could do.

- In stating that Musashi went up to Kyoto following the duel, the *Kōkai fūhansō* seems to go directly against the *Numata kaki* (1672), which claims that Musashi instead went to visit his father in the province of Bungo.

The *Watanabe Kōan taiwa-ki* (1709)

The *Watanabe Kōan taiwa-ki* was written by Sugimoto Yoshichika, a retainer of Maeda Tsunanori (1643–1724). Next to nothing is known of the author of this work, yet thanks to his efforts, we now know all the more about the life of his subject, Watanabe Kōan.

Kōan's father hailed from Settsu, the province that bordered on Harima on the east, but had entered the service of Tokugawa Ieyasu and, in 1582, moved to Suruga (when Ieyasu was put control of the province by Oda Nobunaga in reward for his contribution in subduing Takeda Shingen). Kōan was born shortly afterward and duly entered the service of Ieyasu's son, Hidetada, as the fief's chief of police.

Given Kōan's function he would have spent many an hour in the fief's *dōjō*. And it must have been there that, sometime during the nineties, he first came into contact with famous swordsmen such as Ono Tadaaki and Yagyū Munenori, when the latter entered Hidetada's service as personal fencing instructors. It was probably alongside Tadaaki that Kōan served under Hidetada when the latter launched his ill-advised siege of Ueda castle while on his way along the Nakasendō to join his father in the Battle of Sekigahara.

Where Musashi had declined to enter Hidetada's service as a fencing instructor because the latter had already appointed Yagyū Munenori as his *shihan*, Kōan had no such qualms. Indeed, he became one of Munenori's faithful deshi and remained so until the latter returned to his fief when he was raised to the position of daimyo in reward for his services during the Battle of Sekigahara. Kōan, instead, continued to serve Hidetada in a succession of posts, first as head guard of Fushimi castle, then Sunpu castle, and finally Nijō castle.

During the early twenties Kōan was appointed as a surrogate father to Hidetada's third son, Tadanaga. Born in 1609, Tadanaga proved a precociously gifted child yet plagued by fits of uncontrolled anger. In 1634, Kōan's fatherhood came to an abrupt end when Tadanaga was ordered to commit suicide following an incident in which he killed a retainer in one of his outbursts. After that Kōan became masterless and spent the rest of his life on the road.

And travel he did. His peregrinations not only took him across Japan, but even abroad, to China, Vietnam, Thailand, and as far as India.

Somewhere during the sixties he tired of life on the road. He returned home and entered the service of Maeda Tsunanori, the daimyo of the Kaga fief on the northwest coast of Japan. It was there that he met and befriended the literary talented Sugimoto Yoshichika and asked him to record his travels for posterity. Yoshichika happily obliged and published his work under the name *Watanabe Kōan taiwa-ki*, or *Record of Conversations with Watanabe Kōan*.

In his biography Kōan recounts the experiences he had during his many travels, some of them bordering on the fantastic. Thus de describes how, "on my journey from Vietnam to Thailand I traversed a vast desert in which ships are moved forward by force of wind alone." Such tales, of course, do not lend much credence to his claims concerning Musashi's qualities. Nevertheless, coming from an avowed practitioner of the Yagyū Shinkage school of swordsmanship, Kōan's appraisal of Musashi's strength above that of his own mentor, Munenori, does ring true. His description of Musashi's dislike of water, too, are echoed elsewhere, and the detail with which Musashi's idiosyncratic washing and clothing habits are described add to his account's overall credibility.

❧ Takemura Musashi

I am a deshi of Yagyū Tajima no Kami Munenori and have obtained a license [to practice the Yagyū-ryū]. There was a man by the name Takemura Musashi, famed for having mastered the art of swordsmanship on his own. When compared to master Tajima no Kami, in terms of *go*, Musashi was still the strongest, even if the former were given a nine-stone handicap.

He became the guest of Hosokawa Ettchū no Kami Tadaoki with some thirty servants at his disposal. His son was called Takemura Usaemon and also excelled in various arts. As for Musashi, it goes without saying that he excelled in the martial arts, but he also was a master in all other arts, including poetry, the art of tea, *go*, and *shōgi*.

Yet he had his peculiar flaws. Musashi hated to wash his feet or clean himself with water and never once throughout his life took a bath. Going out on bare feet he would merely wipe them, even if they were soiled. Moreover, since his clothes were dirty, he would wear a velvet coat to disguise the stains. And since he did not care about his physical appearance, even when in front of superiors, he did not spent much time in their presence.

- It is not clear if and when Kōan ever met Musashi in person. If he did it might have been sometime during the first decade of the seventeenth century when, during his protracted stay in Edo, Musashi was invited to Edo castle to give a demonstration in the presence of Tokugawa Hidetada. Though Musashi had declined it is not unlikely that Kōan sought out the famous swordsmen in one of the *dōjō* where he was training.

It is also possible that Kōan met Musashi during the suppression of the Shimabara Rebellion. Both men had taken part in the campaign, Musashi under Ogasawara Tadazane and Kōan under Hosokawa Tadatoshi, the master of Moji castle at the time of Musashi's duel with Sasaki Kojirō on Ganryū Island and later Musashi's host in Kumamoto.

Another, more logical, scenario is that Kōan had known one of Musashi's many deshi and obtained his information from him. One important clue for this version of events is that, while Kōan gets most of the facts about Musashi right, he mistakenly refers to him as "Takemura" Musashi, instead of Miyamoto Musashi—a mistake hardly possible if he had personally met the swordsman. It so happens that one of Musashi's chief deshi went by the name of Takemura Yōemon Yorizumi. The latter had been so close to Musashi that he is often regarded as his third adopted son, and Kōan might understandibly but mistakenly have assumed that Musashi bore the same surname.

Not surprisingly, Yōemon, too, makes his appearance in the *Watanabe Kōan taiwa-ki*. Yōemon had become one of Musashi's deshi during the latter's last years, when he was living in Kumamoto. Shortly before his death Musashi had sent Yōemon to go and instruct his many followers in Nagoya (who were still practicing his Enmei school of swordsmanship) in his more fully developed Niten Ichi school of swordsmanship. That was in 1644, at which time Kōan was still traversing the continent. Yet it might well have been on his return to Japan during the sixties, when Takemura Yōemon was still teaching Musashi's art in Nagoya, that Kōan passed through Nagoya and met with Yōemon. Nagoya castle at that time, after all, was the headquarters of Tokugawa Mitsutomo, daimyo of the Owari fief and, like Kōan, a fervent practitioner of the Yagyū Shinkage school of swordsmanship.

The *Honchō bugei shoden* (1714)

The *Honchō bugei shoden*, sometimes referred to as the *Kanjō shoden*, was written by Hinatsu Shigetaka (1660–1731). Shigetaka was the oldest son of Hinatsu Yoshitada (1625–1686), a retainer of the Matsudaira clan of the Sasayama fief in the province of Tanba.

Hinatsu Yoshitada had immersed himself in the various strands of Saitō Denkibō's Ten-ryū and reunited them in a new style that he called Tendō-ryū. It was on this merit that, sometime during the middle of the seventeenth century, he was hired by Matsudaira Yasunobu as a *shihan* to instruct his clansmen in the Tendō school of swordsmanship.

Apart from studying the Tendō-ryū under his father, Shigetaka also studied other schools, notably the Takeda school of (mounted) archery under Hori Sadanori, who in turn had studied under the famous military strategist Obata Kagenori, author of the *Kōyō gunkan*, the record of the military exploits of the Takeda clan. On the death of his father, in 1686, Shigetaka initially assumed the position as head of his clan and, like his father, served the Matsudaira in the capacity of *shihan*. Yet his studies drew him to the capital and at the turn of the century he decided to move to Edo, where he founded his own school of swordsmanship and diligently pursued his study of the various martial art forms.

Propelled by his deep interest in the great many schools, or *ryūha*, that were practiced in his day, Shigetaka began to compile a record of their origin, their lineages, and the famous *heihōsha* of his day and of times past that stood at their cradle. It was a labor of love, for in the course of his career he managed to collect the biographical data on as many as one hundred fifty noted *heihōsha*, from the early Muromachi period to the early Edo period. In 1714, at the age of 54, Shigetaka decided he had gathered all the information he could find. It took him two more years to compile and edit his material, but finally in 1716 his life's work was published under the title *Honchō bugei shoden*.

Shigetaka's interests ranged wide and far. In describing the arts practiced by its subjects, the *Honchō bugei shoden* covers nine main fields, from the general art of warfare (*heihō*), through the art of archery (*shajutsu*), equestrianism (*bajutsu*), the art of fighting with the spear (*sōjutsu*), the art of fighting with the sword (*kenjutsu*), the art of gunnery (*hōjutsu*), the art of fighting with the *wakizashi* (*kogusoku*), down to the art of combat without weapons (*jūjutsu*), and even the art of etiquette (*shorei*).

And he was well informed. His descriptions of his subjects are vivid, highly anecdotal, and often rich in detail. He was often familiar with his subject's personal backgrounds, even those long dead. Thus he knew that Musashi hailed from the province of Harima, that he belonged to the Shinmen clan, and that his father was Munisai, an expert in the art of fighting with the *jitte*.

The *Honchō bugei shoden* is the oldest such Japanese record and much of what is known today about Japan's great *heihōsha* is drawn from Shigetaka's work. The same is true with respect to Musashi's duels with the Yoshioka brothers. It is, for instance, the first record after the *Kokura hibun* to shed any light on the famous duel between Musashi and the members of the Yoshioka clan. While it is not certain to what extent Shigetaka drew from the *Kokura hibun*, it is clear that subsequent *denki* like the *Bushū denraiki* relied heavily on his work for their portrayal of events.

Among the early authors who wrote on Musashi, Shigetaka is one of the few to name his source, a certain Nakamura

Morikazu. Fortunately, he even mentions that Morikazu was a retainer of Matsudaira Tadahide, and this is where we may possibly trace the source of this vivid account. Matsudaira Tadahide, after all, was the fifth son of Matsudaira Tadakuni, the fifth daimyo to rule the fief of Akashi, where Musashi spent several years advising its daimyo, Ogasawara Tadazane, on the construction of Akashi castle and its town. Since Tadazane had been promoted to the fief of Kokura leaders from different clans had been promoted to the Akashi fief, but in 1649 Tadakuni, who hailed from the province of Tanba, was promoted to Akashi, and remained there until his death in 1659.

It is very likely that Shigetaka's source also hailed from Akashi and was still a young man when, in 1632, Ogasawara Tadazane left Akashi for Kokura. An even more likely scenario would be that Morikazu moved down to Kokura with the rest of Tadazane's retinue and moved back to Akashi at a later stage in his life. That, at least, would account for his vivid account of the events leading up to Musashi's duel on Ganryū Island.

❦ Miyamoto Musashi Seimei

Miyamoto Musashi Seimei hailed from the province of Harima and was a scion of the Shinmen, a strand of the Akamatsu. His father was called Shinmen Munisai and was an adept in the art of the *jitte*. Realizing that the *jitte* was not a common weapon, Musashi, by contrast, always carried two swords as his weapons of combat. Thus it was that he came to use the two swords in favor of the *jitte* and that he gradually perfected this art.

When Musashi was twelve he had a duel with Arima Kihei in Harima, and at the age of sixteen he had a duel with Akiyama, whom he killed. Afterward, in Kyoto, he arranged to have a duel with the Yoshioka, which he duly won. After that he killed Ganryū on the island of Funashima. All in all he took part in some sixty bouts from the age of twelve.

He called his style of swordsmanship the Hinoshita Kaizan Shinmei Miyamoto Musashi Seimei-ryū. His fame was known throughout the country and his reputation has become part of oral tradition. Even now there are tributaries in various provinces. During the Keichō era he was famed for his part in the siege of Osaka castle, and during the Kanei era he went into battle with the Hosokawa. He passed away on the nineteenth day of the fifth month of the second year of the Shōhō era [13 June, 1645]. His Buddhist name was Genshin Niten.

- Hinatsu Shigetaka is the first author to introduce the name "Seimei." It is not clear where he acquired the name, for it is found in no other source except in Masaki Teruo's *Tōsakushi* and Yabuki Masanori's somewhat wrongheaded *Mimasaka ryakushi*, which almost certainly followed Shigetaka's example. Neither Musashi himself, nor any of the other records ever refer to Musashi by this name. Indeed, they quite generally refer to him as Miyamoto Musashi Genshin.
- The *Honchō bugei shoden* is the only extant record to refer to Musashi's school of swordsmanship by the name of Hinoshita Kaizan Shinmei Miyamoto Seimei-ryū. It is not clear where this name originated. It may have been used by one of his many followers, and Shigetaka might have read it in one of the many old documents he encountered in his research, or he might have made it up.

☯ The Yoshioka Clan

The Yoshioka was a clan from Heianjō [Kyoto]. They were masters in the art of swordsmanship, who served as *shihan* to house of Muromachi [Ashikaga] at the so-called Heihōsho. A man named Gion Tōji acquired the deeper secrets of swordsmanship, and the Yoshioka in turn inherited this art of swordsmanship. That is to say the Yoshioka were practicing a strand in the tradition of the schools of Kiichi Hōgen and the Kyōhachi-ryū. It is said that among Kiichi's followers were eight (*hachi*) monks of the Kurama temple in Kyoto. Thus it was that their school of swordsmanship came to be known as the Kyōhachi-ryū.

Now the Yoshioka arranged a duel with Miyamoto Musashi. Both adepts were to meet in duel to decide which of them was the greatest swordsman.

During his duel with the Yoshioka, Musashi wore a crimson hand cloth as *hachimaki*. The Yoshioka swordsman wore a *hachimaki* from a white hand cloth. the Yoshioka swordsman hit Musashi on the brow with his *tachi*. And when Musashi, too, struck the swordsman on the forehead, it was immediately visible, as he was wearing a white *hachimaki*, whereas since Musashi, wore a crimson *hachimaki*, it took some time before the blood on his forehead could be seen. Now the Yoshioka swordsman struck Musashi with a long *bokutō*. Musashi parried the blow, but his *hachimaki* was torn and fell to the ground. Musashi now advanced on the swordsman and cut through the leather *hakama* the latter was wearing. Thus the Yoshioka swordsman cut through Musashi's *hachimaki*, and Musashi did the same with the swordsman's *hakama*. It was a sight to behold, both dazzling to the eye and to the ear, and it was hard to say which of the two adepts had come out on top.

According to another account the Yoshioka swordsman was still wearing his hair on his forehead and had thus not yet reached the age of twenty. He was in the company of one deshi and arrived at the place of duel before Musashi, and leaning on his long *bokutō*, he awaited Musashi's arrival. At length Musashi arrived in a bamboo palanquin and got out of the palanquin at corner close to the place of duel, took out two swords from a bag, wiped them on the bag, and stepped out in front of his adversary carrying one in each hand. The Yoshioka swordsman struck Musashi with a long *bokutō*. Musashi parried the blow, but his *hachimaki* was cut and fell to the ground, while Musashi cut through the swordsman's *hakama*. It was hard to say which of the two adepts had come out on top, but it was a sight to behold, both dazzling to the eye and to the ear.

Again, yet another account claims that while Musashi was indeed apt to use two swords, he invariably used only one sword in duel, never resorting to two. And so, according to this account, it was with his duel with the Yoshioka swordsman.

It is hard to say which of these accounts is true. And while there may be many errors in the way this account has been passed on by word of mouth, all one can do is rely on what one has heard and record the little one knows.

- Gion Tōji was a swordsman who lived during the Muromachi Period (1336–1573). He is believed to have

taught Yoshioka Kenpō, founder of the Kyōhachi-ryū Yoshioka *dōjō*.
- Kiichi (also Oniichi) Hōgen was a legendary court official from the late Heian and early Kamakura period. He is said to have lived along the then capital's Hori River and to have been the instructor of none other than Minamoto no Yoshitsune, one of the most popular warriors of his era. Hōgen was a fervent practitioner of *bun-bu*, the dual practice of the martial and the civil way and an authority on The Six Secret Teachings, a Chinese classic on civil and military strategy. The name of Kiichi Hōgen makes its first appearance in the *Gikei-ki*, a Japanese war-tale from the early Muromachi Period (1336–1573), which records in graphic detail the heroic deeds of Yoshitsune and his men.
- In Edo Japan, when a boy came of age (*genpuku*), he would go through a special ceremony in which his forehead would be shaved and he would receive his adult name. Though twenty was a typical age at which the ceremony was held, it varied from clan to clan and region to region.

❧ The Duel on the Island of Funashima

Nakamura Morikazu said that "according to the words of an old man a long time ago, when the day of the duel between Ganryū and Miyamoto Musashi arrived, a large number of people, regardless of their rank and stature, crossed over to Funashima to witness the event.

Ganryū, too, went to the place where the boats were moored, boarded a boat, and addressed the oarsman saying: "A lot of boats are crossing over today. What on earth is going on." The oarsman replied: "Don't you know? Today is the day that a swordsman by the name of Ganryū is to duel with Miyamoto

Musashi! It is to witness the event that they have been crossing over since the break of day."

Then the swordsman said: "I am that Ganryū you speak of." At this the oarsman was greatly surprised. Speaking under his breath he said: "If you are the said Ganryū, let me cross you over to another place, for you had better quickly make your escape to another province. Even though your technique may be divine, there are a great number of Musashi's friends. Surely, you will not be able to get out alive."

To this the swordsman replied: "I do not desire to outlive today in such a way. Even if I am bound to die as you say, I have made a solemn oath and I would not be a brave warrior if I were to break my promise. If it is my duty to die on Funashima, it is your duty to pour some water on my grave for the repose of my soul, for even though you are merely a lowly oarsman, I am touched by your compassion."

In this manner they reached Funashima. Ganryū jumped out of the boat and waited for Musashi, and the latter, too, arrived on the island, so that finally the moment of duel had been reached. Ganryū fought courageously with all his might, brandishing his sword with the speed of lightning, yet tragically lost his life on Funashima.

Nakamura Morikazu, who was a retainer of Matsudaira Tadahide, was also known by the name of Juroemon. He was an adept in the art of swordsmanship as well as *jūjutsu*.

According to one account, when Musashi crossed over to Funashima, he asked his oarsman to give him an oar and, drawing his *wakizashi*, proceeded to carve away at its grip so as to make it thinner, and leaving the boat, used it in the duel that followed. It is also said that Ganryū fought with a three-foot-long *tachi* that he had named his *monohoshi-zao*, or wash-line rod. Ganryū's grave is still on the island of Funashima.

- Matsudaira Tadahide (1640–?) was the fifth son of Matsudaira Tadakuni (1595–1659), who was promoted to the fief of Akashi in 1649.
- In Japan clothes were traditionally and are still hung out to dry on long bamboo poles called *monohoshi-zao*.

The *Bushō kanjō-ki* (1716)

The *Bushō kanjō-ki* was written by Kumazawa Itarō. Born in 1629, the young Itarō grew up in the port town of Hirado, the place that had been the port of call of the Dutch traders until 1641, when they were forced to move their factory to the island of Deshima in the port of Nagasaki.

Itarō was born into a clan of retainers to the fourth daimyo of the Hirado fief, Matsura Shigenobu (1622–1703), so that when he came of age he was destined to enter the service of his lordship, as his father had done. The young Itarō, however, had other plans; he left Hirado and traveled to the province of Bizen, where he became a pupil of the famous Neo-Confucianist Kumazawa Banzan. Itarō must have been a devoted pupil, for it was from Banzan that he took his new family name. His Buddhist names were Tanan and Saigyokuken, and his posthumous name was Masaoki.

Though it purports to be a celebration of famous warriors or war heroes who had been commended (*kanjō*) for their service by their masters, the *Bushō kanjō-ki* is essentially a collection of biographical or anecdotal tales that Itarō had heard or read in the course of his studies. Thus it includes the anecdote describing how Toyotomi Hideyoshi came to recruit a young Ishida Mitsunari after the latter had served him tea during his stay at a temple.

Musashi makes his appearance in the tenth and last scroll, which also features accounts of a number other famous martial artists including Yoshioka Kenpō, Toda Seigen, Terazawa Hanpei, and Anazawa Morihide.

❦ The Duel between Miyamoto Musashi and Ganryū

Miyamoto Musashi preferred to fight with two swords. He served Hosokawa Tadatoshi, and when he came down from Kyoto to Kokura in Buzen, a swordsman by the name of Ganryū awaited him at Shimonoseki and made it known to him that he wanted to meet him in duel. Musashi agreed and asked the skipper for an oar which he broke in two, cutting a grip on both for his hands, making the longer two-and-a-half feet, and the shorter just under two feet in length. Leaving the boat he fought with Ganryū, who was wielding a three-foot sword, while all those who dwelled in Shimonoseki came to watch.

Musashi crossed his two swords and advanced when Ganryū struck out at him by bringing his sword down in a large arc from above, but Musashi parried the attack and struck Ganryū on the head. The latter now swung round and struck Musashi on the left shoulder. Encouraged, Ganryū moved in and lashed out at Musashi horizontally. But Musashi leapt into the air, pulling up his legs, so that only three inches of his *hakama* was cut off and fell to the ground. At this point Musashi struck out with all his might, breaking Ganryū's skull, who expired instantly. A grave was erected for Ganryū and it is still there today.

- Musashi, of course, did not serve Hosokawa Tadatoshi (1586–1641), but was merely his guest, first at Moji castle during his famous duel on Ganryū Island, and again in Kumamoto during the last years of his life.

🌀 The *Dōbō goen* (1720)

The *Dōbō goen* was written by Shoji Katsutomi, the sixth generation descendant of Shoji Jineimon, the founder of the Yoshiwara pleasure quarters in Edo.

Consisting of two scrolls, the *Dōbō goen* is chiefly a detailed account of the origin and history of the Yoshiwara. Thus Katsutomi describes how in 1612 his ancestor, Jineimon, a leader among early brothel owners, petitioned the Tokugawa shogunate for the exclusive rights to operate brothels in one restricted area in Edo. It took five years for the Bakufu to respond, but in March 1617 Jineimon was finally awarded a piece of land on Edo's outskirts. One-and-a-half years later, in November 1618, the Yoshiwara pleasure quarters finally opened for business and remained so until 1958 when prostitution was outlawed.

The *Dōbō goen*, however, is also an account of Yoshiwara's famous courtesans and their many lovers. And it is in this context that Musashi makes a brief but interesting appearance. When describing the various courtesans of the establishment of Kawai Kenzaemon in Shinmachi, Katsutomi writes that among them "was a courtesan by the name of Kumoi who had a liaison with Miyamoto Musashi."

🌀 Musashi and Kumoi

Among the women of Kawai Kenzaemon in Shinmachi there was a *tsubone* prostitute who a this time became friendly with the adept in the art of fighting with two swords, Miyamoto Musashi, causing her to visit the brothel of Jinzaburō in the same quarter.

During the summer of the fifteenth year of Kanei [1638] there was a rebellion in Shimabara in the province of Bizen. The western daimyo were assigned the task of its suppression and since Miyamoto, too, was going down there as a guard under the command of the house of Kuroda, Jinzaburō visited Kumoi's brothel, where they made preparations for Musashi's departure. Musashi had promised her two spoons by way of practical gifts. He had asked Kumoi to sew a bag of silk crepe for the spoons to which he had attached a piece of blue satin damask. Kumoi, in turn, made him wear a deep red *kosode* from the hide of a young deer with battle *haori* made of black satin.

While there were many high-class prostitutes on display in the latticed brothels, a great crowd gathered at the center of Shinmachi to see this Musashi take his leave. It was an age of ostentation, and it is said that, without ever faltering Musashi spoke felicitous words of farewell to the gathered crowd, mounted his horse outside the great gate and dashed off.

- Katsutomi's claim that Musashi took part in the suppression of the rebellion as a guard is correct. His claim that he did so under the command of the Kuroda, however, is not. Musashi was assigned to an escort to Ogasawara Nagatsugu, the young son of Ogasawara Tadazane, the lord of Musashi's second adopted son, Iori.
- Though one of the few, Katsutomi is not the only author to touch on Musashi's relations to the opposite sex. The *Bushū denraiki* claims that "when Musashi reached old age he had an affair with a woman, who bore him a girl." Its author, Tanji Hōkin, claims he "did not even hear whether he buried the remains, for throughout his life Musashi never again talked about the baby girl."

There are good reasons why Hōkin should be the only one to mention of this tragic episode. One reason is suggested by Hōkin himself, when he asserts that Musashi never again mentioned the deeply painful event to anyone. Other reasons for Musashi's reticence might be the type of liaison that produced the child and it being born out of wedlock. Hōkin describes the woman as an *omoimono*, a word that can mean either a loved one or a prostitute, but sources such as Katsutomi's *Dōbō goen* suggest that the woman who was the object of Musashi's affections belonged to the latter. And while it was quite normal in Musashi's day for men to frequent the pleasure quarters of Edo and the like, a child that was the product of such relationships was an embarrassment. It is only to Musashi's credit that he loved the child. Yet it is also understandable that if Musashi's other early biographers were even aware of the liaison and its result they balked at committing it to paper. All of them, after all, were his disciples by descent and their chief aim was to extol the virtues of the master, rather that expose his weaknesses, however human.

Writing in 1720, seven years before Hōkin completed his own work, Katsutomi cannot have had any knowledge of the *Bushū denraiki*, nor is it, given the geographical divide, likely that Hōkin had read the *Dōbō goen*. We cannot be sure, either, whether Kumoi was the mother of the unfortunate child or whether she was one of Musashi's other mistresses.

The *Koro usawa* ⁽¹⁷⁴⁰⁾

The *Koro usawa* is a work from the hand of the the Edo native Kashiwazaki Eii (17??–1772). Next to nothing is known about Eii, except that he was the author of a number of so-called *zuihitsu* (literally, "follow the brush"), collections of casually recorded thoughts on any topic, among them the *Kokon enkakurō* and the *Jiseki gakkō*, which includes an account of the evacuation of Edo castle during Toyotomi Hideyoshi's campaign against Odawara castle.

Musashi and Yoshioka Kanefusa

Musashi met in duel with Yoshioka Kanefusa at Kitano's Shichihonmatsu. They had both agreed to do so at the fifth hour of dawn. Kanefusa rose early and arrived at Kitano at the appointed hour. Yet Musashi failed to appear, even by midday.

And thus Kanefusa sent round a messenger to where Musashi was staying. Finding that Musashi was still asleep, the messenger pressed Musashi, saying: "Please hurry and keep your appointment with my master." Musashi replied: "Very well," but went on sleeping. When asked by his attendant Musashi replied: "I am trying to think by what strategy I can gain victory, but I am not yet satisfied. I'll go presently."

When he finally arrived at Kitano he was simply dressed in a *hakama* and a *kataginu*. The Yoshioka reproached him and said: "You have made us wait!" But Musashi replied: "I am late as I am ill and my body is not in good shape."

At length the duel commenced. Both men clashed, Kanefusa brandishing a *bokutō*, and Musashi a *shinai*. Musashi struck Kanefusa on his left temple; Kanefusa hit Musashi on the backside of his left shoulder. Such then was Musashi's strategy: to break the Kanefusa's fighting spirit by showing up late.

- The *Koro usawa* is the only record to mention the name Kanefusa, which might have been an alternative name of one of the many Yoshioka brothers.
- Kitano's Shichihonmatsu, literally: "Kitano's seven pine trees," might well be a reference to Shichihonmatsu-doori, one of Kyoto's main thoroughfares just east of the famous Kitano Tenman-gū shrine.

The *Kōkō zatsuroku* (1751)

The author of the *Kōkō zatsuroku* was Matsudaira Kunzan (1697–1783), the fourth son of an Owari retainer by the name of Chimura Hidenobu. A highly intelligent child, he was influenced by his mother (the grandchild of the Confucianist Hori Kyōan) to dedicate himself to a scholarly life and began studying Confucianism and geography.

At the age of thirteen his precocious talents were spotted by Matsudaira Hisatada, a retainer of Tokugawa Tsugutomo (1692–1731), then lord of the fiefdom of Owari (in today's Aichi province). Convinced of the young boy's potential Hisatada accepted him as the future spouse of his then five-year-old daughter, a marriage that was officially sealed in 1712, when Kunzan reached the age of sixteen, thereby technically enrolling him in the service of the powerful Tokugawa. When in 1724 his adoptive father died, Kunzan inherited his father's (reduced) stipend of 250 *koku* and became a member of Tsugutomo's mounted guard. Though it was still a great honor to be counted among a daimyo's mounted guard at the time, it was chiefly a titularly function and, being very much the scholarly type, Kunzan might well have never seen the world from the back of a horse.

In 1743 Kunzan's could finally begin to apply his real talents when he was appointed *kakimono bugyō*, the magistrate in charge of the fiefdom's archive, a post he was to occupy for the next thirty-eight years. It was the perfect function for the now forty-seven-year-old scholar, for he had been collecting all manner of books, scrolls, and documents from the moment he had entered Tsugutomo's service. Using the authority of his newly won position he began to compile an archive under the name of *Shiantei*, or the *Hidden Arbor of History*, which by the end of his tenure had grown to include more than 3700 works. A prolific author as well, Kunzan mined his huge archive to compile some sixty-two works on subjects as diverse as history, topography, poetry, literature, herbalism, and philosophy.

Kunzan not only drew from his archive. To collect his herbs, record local stories, or make his topographies, he travelled the length and breadth of Owari, a fief of close to sixty-two thousand *koku* and straddling the provinces of Owari, Mino, Mikawa, and Shinano. One fruit of his labors was published in 1751 under the title *Kōkō zatsuroku*, a work in ten volumes in which he recorded the experiences and memories of the fief's retainers, some of whom had been born when Musashi was still alive.

Though more than a century had passed by the time Kunzan put pen to paper the intimate knowledge of the archive that he acquired over the course of his career gives considerable credence to his claim that during the Osaka campaign Musashi was fighting among the troops of Mizuno Katsunari. The original copy of Kunzan's work has long since been lost, but a handwritten copy is still kept in Nagoya's municipal archives.

❷ Miyamoto Musashi

Miyamoto Musashi was a man famed for his *heihō*, who acquired the art of swordsmanship at the age of fourteen or fifteen. His father was called Muni, an adept in an art of swordsmanship called the Hachi Koryū. By the time Musashi came to serve Lord Ieyasu, he had already risen to fame by dueling with Yoshioka Seijūrō at the age of eighteen, and with Ganseki at the age of twenty.

During the siege of Osaka castle, when he was fighting with the troops of Mizuno Hyūga no Kami, he carried a five-yard banner on which in bold characters was written the slogan: "Men from the realm of Shakya knew and practiced the laws of Buddha; we know and practice the laws of *heihō*." I do not remember exactly where it was, but at one stage he was standing on a bridge, brandishing his long *bokutō*, and being cheered on as he cast the enemy troops off the bridge left and right.

- The excerpt in question relates to the fighting around Osaka castle during the summer campaign as experienced by the troops under the command of Mizuno Katsunari (1564–1651). On June 2, 1615, Katsunari's troops (which were part of a Tokugawa force of some thirty-eight thousand troops advancing on Osaka from Yamato province) were intercepted by a vanguard of some three thousand men under the command Gotō Mototsugu at a place called Dōmyōji, some ten miles southwest of Osaka. Heavy fighting ensued in which Mototsugu was eventually killed and Katsunari's men prevailed.

  Where the *Kōkō zatsuroku* isn't clear about the precise place and time of the event it describes, an excerpt from the *Mizuno Katsunari oboegaki*, the personal diaries of Mizuno Katsunari, help us to pinpoint the time and place of the described events. Casting his mind back to the days leading up to the summer siege of Osaka castle, Katsunari recalls how:

  > Driving down one flank of the mountain we pursued and crushed the Gotō forces and since both sides of the path were deep with mud, there was a small stone bridge amid the rice paddies. I was the first to mount

> the bridge, followed by Nakayama Kageyu, Mizuno Katsushige, and Murase Saba, and passing the bridge, we drove back the forces of Honda Sakyō, and since the latter also fled into the paddies flanking the bridge, we dismounted from our horses and taking our lances, pursued the enemy all the way back to Fujiidera.

Not surprisingly, being a record describing his own feats and those of his clan members, the *Mizuno Katsunari oboegaki* only mentions the main participants in the battle. Naturally they would have been leading large numbers of troops over the bridge in their pursuit of the enemy. Knowing that Musashi was one of the ten mounted guards attached to the seventeen-year-old Katsushige, it is safe to assume that the events as described by the *Kōkō zatsuroku* are those that took place on the bridge near Dōmyōji on the sixth of May in the twentieth year of the Keichō era (June 2, 1615).

Indeed, it may well have been Nakayama Kageyu, the second retainer to follow Katsunari, whose recollections were passed down to his sons and their sons to finally be recorded by Matsudaira Kunzan when he visited Kageyu's descendants to record their history. It was among the archives of the Nakayama clan, after all, that one of the two roll calls (*Osaka ojin no otomo*) carrying Musashi's name was discovered (see note below).

- Oddly enough, while the popular view (especially in the West) is that Musashi fought on the side of the Toyotomi forces (i.e., the castle's defenders) there is no historical data to support such a view. Perhaps chiefly to blame is the author Yoshikawa Eiji (1892–1962), who in his epic novel *Musashi*, cast Musashi on the side of the western, losing, forces of Ishida Mitsunari (1559–1600) during the decisive Battle of Sekigahara (1600).

One reason for Eiji to have done so might have been to heighten dramatical tension; to have Musashi fight on the losing side, after all, provided the consummate novelist with far more scope for character development than having him among the victors. Yet there is no record to support Eiji's scenario. Indeed, the *Bushū denraiki*, the only record to mention Musashi's whereabouts while Japan's future was being decided at Sekigahara, clearly states that he was taking part in the sieges of Aki and Tomiku castle on the southern island of Kyushu under the command of Kuroda Yoshitaka (1546–1604).

Eiji might have based this version of events on the knowledge that, in order to raise enough troops, the Toyotomi generals mobilized more than a hundred thousand *rōnin*, and since Musashi was generally considered a *rōnin*, his desire to cast Musashi on the losing side might have felt justified. Having accepted that Musashi fought against Ieyasu's forces at Sekigahara it was only logical to assume that he did the same during the siege of Osaka castle.

This, however, is to ignore evidence to the contrary. And in contrast to the above view, there is ample and sound evidence to support the view that Musashi actually fought on the side of the Tokugawa forces under the command of Mizuno Katsunari (1564–1651). Apart from his appearance in the *Kōkō zatsuroku*, Musashi's name appears on a roll call of men who fought under Katsunari titled *Osaka ojin no otomo*. This record was rediscovered in 1984 among the possessions of a certain Nakayama Fumio (Nagoya), a direct descendant of Nakayama Shigemori (Shōgen), who was one of Katsunari's chief retainers.

It is said many years after the siege, somewhere during the Kan'ei era (1624–29) Musashi visited Mizuno Katsunari at his castle at Fukuyama. During his visit he stayed at the *yashiki* of Nakayama Shigemori, who held a banquet in honor of his guest. A certain stone there had become Musashi's favorite place to sit while sojourning in his host's garden. Though Shigemori's *yashiki* has long since been destroyed, the stone has been moved to the precincts of the Bingo Go-kuni shrine, situated on the castle ground's northern perimeter, where it graces the shrine grounds under the name of Musashi Meisō Ishi (Musashi's Meditative Stone).

The *Osaka join no otomo* is not the only roll call to mention Musashi's name in connection to the siege. A similar roll call, kept among the archives of Fukuyama castle confirms that Musashi was one among the 230 mounted warriors (in addition to some 4300 warriors on foot) mobilized under Katsunari's command. The roll call, titled *Osaka o-jin o-ninzu tsukeoboe*, originally was among the papers of the Oba, a clan of Mizuno retainers from Fukuyama. Today, two copies, one drafted in 1752, the other in 1818 are still kept in the Kagami Yagura, the castle's eastern turret, and both carry the name of a certain Oba Heiba.

Moreover, not only does the *Osaka o-jin o-ninzu tsukeoboe* mention that Musashi was among Katsunari's mounted warriors, it explicitly states that he was the fourth among a group of ten mounted warriors attached to none other than "Sakushū-*sama*," the honorary name of Katsunari's son, Katsushige. Two men among the remaining nine are marked as "taking part as *rōnin*," whereas no such label is put on Musashi.

It should also be mentioned that shortly after the siege Musashi adopted the third (and possibly also the fourth) son of Nakagawa Shimanosuke, who served Katsunari and lost his life during the siege in the capacity of *musha bugyō*, or Magistrate of Warriors.

The *Harima kagami* (1762)

Largely completed in 1762, the *Harima kagami*, which is an eclectic collection of works on the customs, places, and people related to the province of Harima, was written and compiled by Hirano Yōsai, a physician from the village of Hirazu (today a part of the city of Kakogawa). Yōsai was not only at home in medicine, but also well versed in mathematics and astronomy.

The *Harima kagami* is especially informative about Musashi's adopted son Iori. It seems only logical that Yōsai should know so much about Iori, for Hirazu lay only a few miles from the village of Yoneda, the place where Iori was born. Iori spent his early childhood in Yoneda until, sometime during the second decade of the seventeenth century, he encountered Musashi while (according to the *Bukōden*) out fishing for loaches in a local paddy field.

Miyamoto Musashi

Miyamoto Musashi hailed from the village of Miyamoto in the vicinity of Ikaruga in the district of Ittō. From an early age he had a passion for the martial arts, traveling through various provinces on *musha shugyō* and being widely known under the heavens, for he counted many a samurai amongst his numerous acolytes by teaching his school of swordsmanship called Musashi-ryū. Yet Musashi never entered the service of any daimyo.

On one of his travels Musashi visited Akashi and was granted an audience with Ogasawara Tadazane. It was at that time that he took as his adopted son a boy called Iori, who accompanied his lordship when he was transferred to the Kokura estate in the province of Buzen. This adopted son Iori served his lordship in the capacity of great elder on a stipend of five thousand *koku*. it is said that, even now, his descendants serve the Ogasawara as elders on a stipend of three thousand *koku*.

This account of Miyamoto Musashi differs from that of an old man and a practitioner of the art of Feng Shui, who is a native of Hirafuku, in the district of Sayō. I will write on this in a different work.

- Ikaruga is a reference to the old Ikaruga *shōen*, or Ikaruga manor. *Shōen* were tracts of land assigned to shrines, temples, officials, or members of the imperial family. The custom began during the Nara period and continued into the Kamakura period, when almost all land had become *shōen*. By then the *shōen* were administered by *shugo*, manor stewards, who had complete say over what occurred within their manor's boundaries.

  The Ikaruga *shōen* dates back to the end of the sixth century. According to records from the Hōryū temple in Nara, the manor was bequeathed to the temple by Empress Suiko to celebrate a lecture on the *Hoke Shōman sūtra* given by the legendary regent and politician Shōtoku Taishi.
- Sadly most of Yōsai's other writings, including the old man's version of Musashi's background, have been lost.

Miyamoto Iori

A *bushi* by the name of Miyamoto Iori lived in the village of Yoneda. His father was called Jinbei. He used to be a samurai in the service of Bessho Nagaharu, but after the fall of Miki castle, he came to settle in Yoneda, where Iori was born.

When Iori was twelve he went out fishing and, perhaps because he was led astray by a long-nosed goblin, lost his way and ended up in the vicinity of Kakogawa. At that moment an incarnation in a white costume grabbed the young boy by his sleeve and led him back to the village of Yoneda, yet the incarnation vanished without trace. It is said that until recently the sleeve in question was in the possession of Iori's clan, but that it has sadly been lost.

Later, when Iori reached the age of sixteen, the master of Akashi castle, Ogasawara Tadazane, invited into his service a certain Miyamoto Musashi, a warrior without equal under the heavens. The latter did not enter the lord's service but instead stayed on as his guest. Iori, at this time, was in the service of his lordship, and noticing the young boy's inbred ability and good nature, Musashi adopted him as his son. Later, when his lordship moved down to Kokura in Buzen, Iori went with him. When the Shimabara Rebellion arose, he followed his lordship in battle and distinguished himself. In reward, he received a stipend of three thousand *koku* without a position, although he later became a senior retainer under the name Miyamoto Iori.

Even today, descendants and relatives of Iori's house of Tawara live in Yonemura.

Later, as the Tomari Jinja was his clan's family shrine, Iori completely restored the shrine, including a worship hall, a hall for the performance of court dances, its stage, as well as the entrance gate. The signatures of all the men who had been in charge of reconstruction are engraved in the shrine's stone lanterns and can still be read today. All this was achieved by transporting the structure of the old Tomari shrine to the village of Yoneda where it was used as the main building for a shrine by the name of Uchimiya. Iori also donated various costly artifacts to the Tomari shrine, including a portrait of the *Sanjūrokkasen*. Even now, when his descendants travel up to Edo from Kokura, they interrupt their journeys to worship at the Tomari shrine.

Now master Iori's mother hailed from the village of Miyawaki in the Tarui manor of the Katō district. As a result, Iori spent much of his childhood in the village of Miyawaki.

Also, among Iori's siblings (though in fact he was his nephew) was a man named Miyachō Seibei. In answer to Seibei's long-cherished wish, a votive tablet of the *Sanjūrokkasen* was composed by the *kuge* and written down by the then emperor. It is still kept as a treasure in a small shrine of the Tarui manor.

Another brother of Iori was called Ohara Genshō, whose stone monument is currently in the grounds of the Hoyō temple of the Nichiren sect in Miki village. The right-hand tablet of this monument was donated by Iori and Genshō together.

- From the family records of the Miyamoto clan in Kokura, as well as the *Tomari jinja munefuda*, it is now clear that Iori was indeed a native of Harima, where he was born as the second son of Tawara Hisamitsu, a samurai in the service of Bessho Nagaharu (1558–80), the lord of Miki castle.
- Bessho Nagaharu (1558–80) was a powerful force in the region during the early second half of the sixteenth century. Nagaharu's headquarters were at Miki castle, some thirty

miles south east from Hirafuku, and not far from the port of Akashi on the Inland Sea.

It was during this period that Oda Nobunaga set his mind on subduing western Honshu in his his drive to unify the country. His most powerful adversaries there were the great Mori clan, whose power base lay in the western province of Aki. Nagaharu had initially supported Nobunaga's drive westward, but due to his wife's clan relations, he stubbornly refused to submit to the rule of Toyotomi Hideyoshi, at that time Nobunaga's chief general in the region.

Banding with other local chieftains he began to attack Hideyoshi's forces, even calling in the help of the Mōri. His resistance proved so fierce that at one stage, Hideyoshi's army was forced to retreat, which so enraged the great general that he laid siege to Miki castle. Finally, in January 1580, having held out for a year and ten months, Nagaharu agreed to commit *seppuku* with his wife and children on the condition that those who had served them would be spared.

- One reason why Musashi might have taken a special interest in the young Iori is that his stepmother, Yoshiko, was also of Bessho descent. Her father, Bessho Shigeharu, the master of Rikan castle, had chosen Nagaharu's side in the conflict. In 1578, shortly after Hideyoshi laid siege to Miki castle, a force under the command of Amago Katsuhisa the master of Kōzuki castle, situated only a few miles south of Hirafuku, laid siege to Rikan castle. The castle fell after a few weeks and Shigeharu was dispossessed. That same year, Katsuhisa's domain was in turn overrun by a Mōri alliance, upon which both castles fell into the hands of the Ukita, one of the Mōri's staunchest allies.
- The *Sanjūrokkasen*, or the thirty-six immortals of poetry, were a group of poets of the Nara, Asuka, and Heian periods selected by Fujiwara no Kintō for their exquisite poetic craftsmanship.

🌀 The *Mukashibanashi* (176?)

The one source to shed light on Musashi's stay in Nagoya and the spread there of his Enmei school of swordsmanship is the *Mukashibanashi*, a collection of anecdotes recorded in thirteen scrolls by Chikamatsu Shigenori (1697–1778). Shigenori came from a clan of Owari (today's Aichi prefecture) retainers. Shigenori's father had served the Owari Tokugawa during their stay in Edo (under the *sankin kōtai* system). At a young age Shigenori entered the service of Tokugawa Tsugutomo (1692–1731) in Owari and served most of his life in the latter's *umamawarigumi*, the daimyo's elite household mounted guards.

It was probably in his capacity of *umamawarigumi* that that Shigenori gathered the many anecdotes surrounding Musashi that were passed down by those who had known him during his two-year stay in Nagoya. And while the *Mukashibanashi* cannot be accurately dated, it was probably sometime during the early second half of the eighteenth century that Shigenori committed his gathered recollections to paper.

🌀 Musashi's Visit to Nagoya

When Miyamoto Musashi came to Nagoya, he was invited [by Lord Yoshinao Tokugawa] to demonstrate his art of swordsmanship in his lordship's presence. When his opponent suddenly opened the attack, Musashi crossed his two swords, training the tip of his long sword on the tip of his adversary's nose, thus steadily forcing the latter backward until they had traced the circumference of the whole *dōjō*, and said, "This is the way in which I fight duels." Again he was challenged by one of Lord Tokugawa's retainers, but again Musashi won the contest hands down. It is said that the contest was fought at the hour of the tiger, although it isn't clear who attended the duel.

Afterward, Musashi heard of a man by the name of Nagano Goroemon, one of the clan's retainers, and a master in the Yagyū school of swordsmanship, and called on him to request that they have a *shiai*. Goroemon met with Musashi and welcomed him with the words, "I have long wanted to meet with you and finally you have come." Then they talked at leisure, upon which Goroemon asked, "By the way, Master Musashi, I read the [*Heihō*] *sanjū-go kajō*. Is that one of your writings?" Musashi answered and said, "I see. Yes, it is a tract written by me."

At this Goroemon said, "Forgive me for saying this, but I believe the work is a failure. I would imagine that you now regret having ever written it." Musashi answered, "Indeed, it is an embarrassment. I wrote it when I was still inexperienced and now deeply regret it. Yet, as it has spread throughout the realm and even you have come to read it, I simply am at a loss what to do about it. I am impressed, for you exceed your reputation. You are the only person I have met so far to call it a failure. How good it is to hear someone's unbridled opinion." Speaking like this, Musashi forgot all about the *shiai* and left having had a pleasant conversation and drawing a painting for his host. It is said that at length Musashi left the province of Owari.

During his stay in Owari Musashi won *shiai* in several places. Upset with the idea that Musashi might think that Owari had no good swordsmen, his lordship was greatly pleased when he heard how Musashi had been cornered by Nagano's words. And it is said that this was the reason why Musashi did not enter his lordship's service.

Failing to procure a position with the Owari house of Tokugawa, Musashi left for another place taking the Kiso Highroad, when he stopped at the border and looked back on the region of Owari and said to his travel companions, "When I came to Nagoya this time it would have been better had I not engaged in any duels, but become a deshi of the Yagyū from the start and enter the service of the lord of Owari. Instead, I rashly and ostentatiously went for victory, thereby damaging my own cause. It is a lifelong regret." Who can say what emotions were in his heart at that moment?

- It is highly unlikely that Musashi had already written the *Heihō sanjū-go kajō* (*Thirty-five Articles on the Art of Heihō*) by this time, for it is well documented that Musashi wrote it when he was living in Kumamoto in old age. The *Bukōden*, for instance, claims Musashi wrote the document in the spring of 1641 in response to a request by Lord Hosokawa Tadatoshi. To be true to the text, the *Bukōden* speaks of the *Heihō sanjū-kyū kajō* (*Thirty-nine Articles on the Art of Heihō*) which leaves a possibility that Musashi had written a text consisting of thirty-five articles at an earlier stage in his life and in old age drafted a revised version containing four more articles.

☯ The *Seiryūwa* (1782)

Another source to shed light on Musashi's life in Akashi is the *Seiryūwa*, the private records of Ogasawara Tadazane (1596–1667). In 1616, in the wake of the summer siege of Osaka castle, Tadazane, who was then only twenty years old, was promoted to the newly created fief of Akashi, which produced a hundred thousand *koku* a year.

It was not much later that, through the offices of Honda Tadamasa (1575–1631), the daimyo of the neighboring fief of Himeji, Musashi was introduced to the young Tadazane and became an extraordinary advisor to the daimyo's *zōei bugyō*, the construction magistrate in charge of a new castle and castle town.

The headquarters of the fief of Akashi at that time was still Funage castle, which was outdated and far too small for a domain of such size. For reasons of safety, the Bakufu allowed only one castle to remain standing per domain, and thus Funage and all the smaller strongholds in the domain were demolished to create a new one, many times larger than anything built before.

The foundations for the new Akashi castle were laid along the coast of the Inland Sea, right at the strategic narrows between the mainland and the island of Awaji. From there any hostile traffic through the Straits of Akashi could be stopped before it reached Osaka. A harbor was built for the small fleet of ships that would police the straits, while a newly laid-out castle town was erected to house all the retainers, mariners, merchants, and artisans who in one way or other served the young lord of Akashi castle.

Recorded in 1782, the *Seiryūwa* describes how, following the completion of the castle's main structures, the young lord Tadazane began work on embellishing the new home for himself and his wife and so approached Musashi to design the gardens on his castle grounds.

❷ The Construction of Akashi Castle

Facing the western side of the third ring of Akashi castle was a narrow strip of enclosed land stretching northward. On the part that was barren and uninhabited the lord built a *yashiki* surrounded with trees and shrubs, so it could be used as an area for recreation and the performance of tea ceremonies, and in addition to this, a public bath with adjacent tatami rooms, and a field for playing ball.

He put Miyamoto Musashi in charge of the construction of the tea house, miniature mountains, a miniature lake, a waterfall, as well as the planting of trees and shrubs, and it took one year for the construction work to be completed.

At the time of construction, a huge force of laborers from within the lord's domain was mobilized. A large ship was sent over to the province of Awa and Shodoshima in the province of Sanuki to transport the rocks for the miniature mountain. Trees and shrubs were collected from temples and monasteries around Akashi and Miki, while others were bought at Osaka and Sakai, from where they were shipped to Akashi. At this time his lordship was not obliged to visit Edo, and thus he could do as he wished without trouble.

- Sadly, today the gardens designed by Musashi lie once

again barren. In 1922, during a major redesign of the castle gardens many of the trees, shrubs, and rocks were transferred to create a new garden in the vicinity of the Otome pond, on the castle's southeastern side. After the war, the original gardens were turned into an athletic field and have remained so until the present day. In 2003, to attract more visitors to Akashi castle on the wave of a Musashi boom, the gardens around Otome pond were renamed Musashi Teien, or the Musashi Gardens.

The *Saiyū zakki* (1783)

The *Saiyū zakki* was written by Furukawa Koshōken (1726–1807). Born in the village of Shinpon in the province of Bittchū. Not much is known about his youth, except that he lost his mother at the age of eight and that he moved to Kyoto at the age of twenty. Well known, however, is that from an early age he had a great fondness for traveling. Later he settled in the vicinity of Arai (today's Kurashiki), There he opened a pharmacy, yet due to a fondness for gambling he developed huge debts for which at one stage he was sued.

After he reached the age of fifty he began to write down his travel experiences, perhaps with a view toward paying off his debtors. The first fruit of his labors was the *Saiyū zakki*, an account of his solitary travels around the island of Kyushu, written when he was fifty-eight. Five years later he wrote a similar account of his travels to the northern regions of Honshu, this time in the company of a team of Bakufu inspectors.

It was on the outset of his travels around the island of Kyushu that Koshōken passed the Straits of Shimonoseki and visited Ganryū Island (Funashima), backdrop of the famous duel between Musashi and Sasaki Kojirō (Ganryū, according to Koshōken).

It might have been his relations with the Bakufu officials struck up on his travel north that eventually helped Koshōken into a position as geographical surveyor for the Bakufu. In 1794 he carried out a comprehensive survey of Musashi province, submitting a map of the province accompanied by a detailed report the next year. The next year he returned to his home village of Shinpon, which lay in the Okada fief of the Itō clan. In reward for his services his lord Itō Nagatomo (1764–1850) gave Koshōken permission to bear a surname and to carry two swords, promoting him effectively to the upper social class of samurai. It is not likely that he often wore his swords, let alone used them, for by now he had reached the respectable age of seventy.

It seems that, like the great Matsuo Basho, Koshōken preferred an ascetic life over one of luxury. Thus, in the autumn of the year he had become a septuagenarian (*koki*), a significant age in Japanese culture, Koshōken built a bamboo hut in his garden, where he spent much of the twilight of his years in quiet meditation. Koshōken died in 1807 at the age of eighty-two, leaving behind a large number of travelogues, tales, and collections of notes.

The Duel on Ganryū Island

Ganryū Island was originally called Funashima, until a dispute between Miyamoto Musashi and Sasaki Ganryū ended in a duel on this island in which Ganryū was killed by Musashi. Those who had known Ganryū erected a grave for him on the island, which was renamed Ganryū Island.

What is passed on by those who live in Shimonoseki greatly differs from what is written in books. Having arranged to duel with Musashi, Ganryū crossed over to Funashima in a small boat from Izaki, at which point he was accosted by the port's people, who said: "Musashi has crossed over to the island with a large following, so that you are greatly outnumbered. There is no way you can beat them on your own. We beg you not to cross over today." At this Ganryū said: "A *bushi* cannot renege on his words. I made a solid promise, so I would put all *bushi* to shame if I did not cross over today. If they were to kill me using great numbers the shame would be theirs." And having spoken, he crossed over to the island. And indeed, four of Musashi's *deshi* had formed a band and killed Ganryū.

The villagers who had accosted Ganryū were touched by Ganryū's grave sense of justice and therefore called the island Ganryū Island once they had erected his grave. I don't know if it is true or not, but I have just recorded the story as it is passed on by the locals, so that those who come after us can hear it. Others say that Musashi's descendants dwell among those who live in Kokura and that he too has a grave, which stands opposite that of Ganryū.

- Koshōken is not the only one to claim that Musashi's deshi had a hand in the death of his opponent. The *Numata kaki*, for instance, claims that "Following the duel Kojirō regained consciousness, yet Musashi's deshi ganged up on him and killed him." In yet other accounts Musashi's opponent is only warned of the danger of Musashi's accomplices, such as in the *Honchō bugei shoden*, according to which the oarsman who ferries the rival over to the island warns him that: "There are a great number of Musashi's friends. Surely, you will not be able to get out alive." All accounts, however, seem to confirm that Musashi won the duel.

The *Gekken sōdan* (1790)

The *Gekken sōdan* was written by Mikami Genryū, son of a financial officer to the Ikeda clan of the Okayama fief in the province of Bizen, bordering Harima on the west and Mimasaka on the south. His father was often required to travel to Edo, occasions on which he would take the young Genryū with him.

Stepping into his father's footsteps Genryū entered the service of the Ikeda and was often required to travel—during the course of which he began to collect a vast amount of records on the multitude of different schools of combat that were being practiced in his day. Just how much work went into the compilation of the *Gekken sōdan* is borne out by the preface Genryū added to his work when, in 1790, it was finally published:

> Counting back from this year, the second year of Kansei, I have spent some twenty years in this pursuit. During that time I collected, among others, accounts of how various *ryūha* performed in some of the most significant duels, amounting to some one hundred entries in all. Or, given that there were also those who, for reasons of their particular standing among their peers, were apt to divulge the inner secrets of a certain school, I would indulge such persons in their preferred way and leave it to them to recall what they could so that I could record it for posterity.

Together with Hinatsu Shigetaka, author of the *Honchō bugei shoden*, Genryū is one of the few authors to name one of his sources, in his case (a copy of?) the *Heidō kagami*, a short treatise on the art of swordsmanship Musashi had written when still living in Edo and developing his Enmei-ryū (see the chapter on the *Sōkyū-sama o-degatari*). Spending the bigger part of his working life in the pursuit of similar sources, Genryū compiled a veritable treasure trove of information on the various *ryūha* and *heihōsha* of his time and times gone by.

❧ The Musashi-ryū

The Musashi-ryū is the school of swordsmanship of Miyamoto Musashi no Kami Yoshitsune.

Master Musashi was born in the village of Miyamoto in the Yoshino district of Mimasaka province. His father was called Shinmen Munisai and was an adept with the *jitte*. Musashi practiced this art, but was troubled by the thought that the *jitte* was not a weapon commonly used.

He came to realize the importance of a technique by which he could defeat his enemy using the two swords that were always in his belt. And thus he invented a new style of combat and came up with a school of swordsmanship that used both swords. He subsequently traveled the provinces acquiring fame for this school of swordsmanship.

When he dueled with the man named Ganryū he asked the oarsman who ferried him across for some bamboo poles, which he used as his two swords, while Ganryū fought with a real sword. In the end Musashi won the duel and Ganryū was slain.

❧ The Gan-ryū

The Gan-ryū was a school of swordsmanship practiced by the man named Ganryū who, as I mentioned above, dueled with Miyamoto Musashi. Though one should speak of the "Ganryū-ryū," it has become common to refer to it as the Gan-ryū. Even today this school of swordsmanship is widely practiced on the island of Shikoku. In other provinces, too, the school's name can be heard here and there.

One of the techniques of this school is the so-called *isshin ittō*. In this technique one walks right up to one's opponent while holding the large sword in front as if one were about to bring it straight down on his head and then, aiming for the tip of his nose, bringing it down to the ground in an instant. No sooner has one struck out than one moves in on the opponent, stooping down, and achieving victory by lifting him up from his legs as he is about to strike from above. A man by the name of Otani Shinsaemon from the fief of Tottori in the province of Inaba is a *shihan* in this school of swordsmanship.

According to one account, in the latter days of the shogun's court in Kyoto, Musashi went up to the capital and dueled with the Heihōsho's Yoshioka Kenpō and defeating the latter, he received from the shogun the title "First Under the Heavens," a title, it should be noted, that brought him fame throughout the realm. It is said that during his duel with this Kenpō, as well as that with Ganryū, he used only one sword.

Whether these accounts are true or not, we can still find the seal bearing this title among the licenses of this school of swordsmanship, as well as the name Tenka-ichi Miyamoto Musashi Yoshitsune. While the song "Musashi Musō" is already well known among the villagers, when one goes into the mountains it is known by all, and it is also recorded at the end of one of the school's manifests called *Heidō kagami*.

❧ The Duel

According to another account, when Miyamoto Musashi and Sasaki Ganryū decided to meet in duel, both their deshi grew fearful and were full of doubt. One of Musashi's deshi by the name of Yamada spoke with one of Ganryū's deshi by the name of Ichigawa and they both began to boast of their master's strengths. Yamada spoke and said, "Musashi mentioned that your master particularly favors the long sword, but he has prepared a *bokutō*, saying that he will gain victory by utterly crushing him." At this Ichikawa said, "The sword you speak of is not just any sword; it is the sword that Ganryū calls the tiger-killing sword. Since this sword will gain those who wield it victory, regardless who their opponent is, my master will surely gain victory."

Yamada now quickly hurried back to Musashi's side and recounted to him the conversation he had had with Ganryū's deshi. Musashi replied, "I have heard of this tiger-killing sword. I trust it is so." Thus came the day of their duel, and while he let Ganryū kill as many tigers as he would, Musashi, nimble and agile as he was, nevertheless gained victory by leaping up in the air and striking him on the brow, even though the hem of his leather *hakama* had been cut.

- The *Gekken sōdan* is the first record to claim that Musashi hailed from the province of Mimasaka, even though, in the opening lines of his *Gorin no sho*, Musashi specifically stated that he was born in the province of Harima. Musashi's claim is backed by the *Honchō bugei shoden* and the *Harima kagami*. It is not clear from where Mikami Genryū gained the notion that Musashi was born in the neighboring province of Mimasaka, as he must have had access to both records, the first of which appeared more than half a century earlier, and the latter of which appeared several decades before. Yet in doing so Genryū set a precedent for a string of records and publications claiming that Musashi was a native of Mimasaka, most notably the *Tōsakushi* and the *Mimasaka ryakushi* (see the notes to the *Tōsakushi* on this subject).

  Vexingly, even Musashi's adopted son Iori fails to shed any clear light on these claims. Thus, in the *Tomari jinja munefuda*, he merely states that, "Among the Akamatsu diaspora of the province of Mimasaka there were those who belonged to a line called the Shinmen," and that Musashi was heir to this house. Even the *Kokura hibun*, which was composed on his request, is vague on the matter, merely stating that Musashi was "a scion of the Shinmen, last descendants of the Akamatsu of Harima."

- Mikami Genryū is also the first biographer to claim that Yoshitsune was part of Musashi's name. It is clear where he got this notion, for in the passage on Musashi's duel with the Yoshioka he claims that the name Musashi Miyamoto Yoshitsune could be found written in the *Heidō kagami*. Today only copies exist of this earliest of records left by Musashi, yet assuming that they were copied correctly, it would mean that Musashi did use the name Yoshitsune at the time he was living in Edo, when he wrote the *Heidō kagami*.

 Late Edo, Meiji Texts
1851–97

The *Tōsakushi* (1851)

The *Tōsakushi* was written by Masaki Teruo, who served Matsudaira Yasuchika, daimyo of the Tsuyama fief in the province of Mimasaka, as an advisor and instructor in the Kōshū-ryū Gungaku, a school of military strategy connected to he house of the great warlord Takeda Shingen.

The *Tōsaskushi* draws heavily from an earlier topography called the *Sakuyōshi*. The initiative for the *Sakuyōshi* came from a certain Nagao Katsuaki, likewise a retainer attached to the Tsuyama fief, but at a time when it was still being ruled by the once so powerful Mori clan. Seeking to comprise the whole of Mimasaka province, the topography was a project of vast proportions. Katsuaki delegated the task to two men, Emura Sōfu, who was to survey Tsuyama's six western districts, and Kawagoe Genmi, who was to do the same for its eastern districts. At that time Tsuyama also still had six eastern districts, the most eastern of which was Yoshino, in which lay the village of Miyamoto.

Emura acquitted himself well and completed his work within a year. Genmi, however, was overwhelmed by the task at hand. He kept putting off the deadline, and when Katsuaki threatened to delegate the task to someone else, Genmi set fire to what he had completed.

Meanwhile, the fortunes of the Mori clan were waning. Lord of Tsuyama castle at the time was Mori Naganari (1671–97). Naganari had become daimyo of Tsuyama at the tender age of sixteen, and it was Katsuaki's task to assist his lord in the management of his vast estate. The young lord, however, was at loggerheads with his uncle, Nagatake, whose role it was to act as Naganari's guardian. Partly to exert his own authority, and partly to spite his uncle, Naganari pursued a policy in support of centralized Bakufu control, a policy that increasingly undermined the power of his clan.

Stuck with an unfinished project, yet without the resources to complete it, Katsuaki decided to make do with what he had, and in 1691 Emura's topography of Tsuyama's six western districts was published under the name *Sakuyōshi*.

The *Sakuyōshi* was the last such project to be issued with the patronage of the Mori in Tsuyama. In the spring of 1697 lord Naganari fell seriously ill. Two months latter, having only reached the age of twenty-seven, he passed away without a son. His nephew, Atsutoshi, who was only three years his junior, was chosen to succeed him as lord of Tsuyama. Frail and with an unbalanced mind, Atsutoshi developed a fever and went mad, cursing the Bakufu and its policies.

All this happened while he was staying in a hostel in Ise on his way to the capital for an audience with the shogun to confirm his succession. Highly sensitive, the young new lord had been traumatized by the forced self-immolation of one of his retainers, who had failed to prevent a gang of *rōnin* from killing a large number of dogs in a kennel under his supervision. When word of this reached the Bakufu, Atsutoshi was immediately relieved from his post. The rest of the Mori clan were transferred to a smaller domain, and the Tsuyama fief was reduced in size, leaving less than half of its previous six eastern districts under its jurisdiction. The next year its new lord, Matsudaira Nobutomi, entered Tsuyama castle as the new daimyo of the Tsuyama fief.

It was with permission of Nobutomi's distant successor, Matsudaira Naritaka, that Masaki Teruo set about to compile a topography of all the six districts that previously belonged to the Tsuyama fief and which had failed to make it into the *Sakuyōshi*. That this entailed a lot of extra work is borne out by the fact that only some forty-five of the three-hundred fifty villages that Teruo visited on his travels fell under Matsudaira control. Thus Yoshino, the district in which lay the village of Miyamoto, now was under direct Bakufu control.

There was good reason why a man allotted such a task should be expert in the field of the military tactics. Though Japan had been at peace for close to two centuries, its society remained a feudal one, and while topographies at the time described aspects as divergent as the geography, weather, culture, people, and history of a specific region, all these aspects were seen, understood, and used from a feudal, i.e, military point of view. As such Masaki Teruo was the perfect man to compile such a topography. A so-called *heigakusha*, a military expert, Teruo was trained in the Kōshū-ryū, the Echigo-ryū, as well as the Yamaga-ryū, the school founded by Yamaga Sokō, the philosopher-strategist who first developed the ethics of *bushidō*.

Teruo set out on his massive task in the spring of 1812. On his travels through the fief's eastern districts he gathered written and oral transmissions on the martial arts and carefully matched them against existing records, works such as the *Kunimoto nikki*, a vast diary of the Matsudaira clan begun in 1804 (and continued until 1830). Another work he drew from was the *Shinmen kaki*, a history of the Shinmen clan that he had transcribed earlier in his career.

Teruo completed a first draft in 1815 under the title *Tōsakushi*, but diligently pursued his forays for another three years and kept adding and editing his labor of love right up until 1823, the year of his death.

Following Teruo's death, his work was presented to the Tsuyama fief, but nothing was done with it, and it seemed destined to gather dust in the fief's archives—until 1851, when the scholar Sakaya Seikei (1792–1858), who had been appointed as the clan's official Confucianist teacher, discovered it in the clan's residence in Edo. The records he found were in a bad state: they were in complete disarray and some were even missing. Impressed with his find Seikei set to work, creating order out of chaos and reverently filling in the lacuna. Finally, his work complete, he issued thirty-one scrolls under the name *Tōsakushi*.

- Yamaga Sokō (1622–85) was a Confucian and military strategist. The son of a masterless samurai from Aizu Wakamatsu, Sōkō was only six when he was sent to Edo, where he entered the Kokunkan, the famous Confucian school of Hayashi Razan, the great Neo-Confucian scholar who served as tutor the first four shoguns of the Tokugawa Bakufu.
    At the age of fifteen Sokō began studying the Kōshū-ryū under the *heigakusha* Obata Kagenori, author of the *Kōyō gunkan*, the record of the military exploits of the Takeda clan. During his early career he toed the Neo-Confucian line set out by Razan, writing a number of works on Confucianism as well as the native Shintō religion in their relation to the warrior class. Aware of the anomalous position of the samurai class in time of peace, he became increasingly concerned to reconcile the (moral) role of the samurai with his philosophical outlook.
    At the age of forty he broke away from the official doctrine and began to work toward a way to codify the samurai's martial ethics and thereby their role in Tokugawa society. He developed the concept of *shidō*, "the way of the warrior," stressing the dual—martial and civil—role of the samurai in his duty to his lord, thus serving as a living example to the rest of society.
- Sakaya Seikei (1792–1858) was a late-Edo poet who had studied Confucianism under Hayashi Jussai (1768–1841), eighth in line after Hayashi Razan.

❂ Miyamoto Musashi's *Yashiki*

Miyamoto Musashi's *yashiki* occupies an area of some three thousand square yards. It is said that, in the fifteenth year of Kanei [1638], in the wake of the Shimabara Rebellion, the stone wall that surrounded it was demolished by order of the authorities. It stood in the shade of a tall zelkova with a circumference of some twenty-seven feet, which can compete with the old tree on the premise of the Aramaki Daimyo shrine [today's Sanomo shrine].

Musashi's family has lived here from the time of his father, Muni (his original name being Hirata, although he is also called Munisai), and even today, each successive generation of descendants lives here.

- Sadly, Musashi's family home was destroyed by fire during the middle of the twentieth century. A new house with a tiled roof has been erected where it once stood, but a memorial stone in its front garden still marks the place where the Miyamoto *yashiki* once stood.

❂ Hirata Muni

Hirata Muni belonged to a remaining strand of the Akamatsu. Or it may have been that Tarōemon, the son of Hirao Gorōzaemon became a *rōnin*, settled in the village of Miyamoto and took on the name of Miyamoto Muni.

Hirata Muni belonged to the house of Shinmen and was a man of great valor who had no equal in meritorious service in war. He was an adept in the art of swordsmanship and had distinguished himself on the field of battle countless times since

Kurui Ōmi no Kami Kagemori invaded the district of Yoshino in the third year of Entoku [1491].

In the seventeenth year of Tenshō [1589] Shinmen Munetsura secretly ordered Muni to slay Honiden Gekinosuke. Besides being Muni's chief deshi, Gekinosuke was guilty of no crime, and thus Muni sternly refused to do any such thing. Munetsura, however, would not take no for an answer, so that, in the end, Muni reluctantly consented. He sent a messenger to Honiden saying, "I will initiate you in the inner secrets of my school of combat. I am growing old, so be sure to come and without tarrying even a day." Gekinosuke was delighted with the message and went to Muni's house at the appointed time.

Now since that day happened to be the day Muni's father had passed away, a monk by the name of Nakatsukasa from the Ryūdō temple (in the working-class neighborhood of Miyamoto) came to administer the rites. Muni took him aside and told him the gist of Munetsura's plot and said: "I am an old man, while Gekinosuke is still a man in his prime, who is intrepid and has great physical strength. If I mess up, please lend me your sword."

While he was speaking to the monk Gekinosuke arrived. Muni offered his guest sake and tea, and when they had done talking, Gekinosuke asked him about his initiation. Muni now led him into another room and took hold of his hand, tightening his grip saying, "This is how one grabs one's opponent's hand according to my school of combat." Muni's grip was so firm that Gekinosuke cried out he was in pain, but when Muni said that he was being arrested on Munetsura's instructions he exerted the fearsome strength for which he was famed. A scuffle ensued upon which Nakatsukasa took a *yari* and pierced Gekinosuke's chest. He thrust the weapon back and forth so that Gekinosuke quickly lost strength, at which point Muni took his head, cruel though it was.

Because of this incident, Gekinosuke's father, Honiden Suruga no Kami, fled to the Awai manor, while Muni was criticized by all who were in Munetsura's service. It is said that after that he withdrew and remained indoors. I do not know the year and month in which Muni died. An old tombstone marks his grave among the Jigami hills, above the Miyamoto *yashiki*.

- The *Tōsakushi* is the first record to claim that Muni's original name was Hirata. It makes sense that Teruo would arrive at this conclusion. Delving around in historical records related the Shinmen clan the historian soon found that the a samurai by the name of Muni had been in the service of the Shinmen, but that his clan name was not Miyamoto, rather Hirata. Thus a warrior by the name of Hirata Muni makes his appearance in the *Shinmen kaki*, the records of the Shinmen clan which Teruo had already uncovered and transcribed earlier in his career.

  Though Teruo's discovery seems to explain the source of the name Shinmen in Musashi's unabreviated name, it is at the same time one of the most contentious aspects in the reconstruction of Musashi's life, for it means that Musashi must almost certainly have been born in the village of Miyamoto in the district of Yoshino in the province of Mimasaka, and that he was therefore not a native of the province of Harima.
- Shinmen Munetsura was the son of Shinmen Munesada, the master of Takeyama castle in the province of Mimasaka. Early in 1554, the domains of Shinmen Munesada were overrun by the forces of Amago Hiruhisa (1514–61), who at that

time controlled no less than eight of Honshu's western provinces. Following the fall of Takeyama castle, the Shinmen were dispossessed. Over the next few decades they made several attempts to recover what they had lost, but all of their efforts proved abortive. Dispossessed and disillusioned Munesada passed away in 1558. The care of Munetsura, who was still in his infancy, was taken over by his uncle.

By the time Munetsura came of age the fortunes of the Shinmen were again waxing. Their first good fortune came with the death, in 1562, of Amago Hiruhisa and then, in 1566, with the fall of their Amago stronghold of Tomida castle. Becoming enfeoffed to the powerful warlord Ukita Naoie, Munetsura gradually restored the standing of his clan in the region so that during the eighties and nineties, the Shinmen held possessions in the Yoshino district totaling some five thousand *koku*, had some sixty samurai in their service, and employed close to two hundred men and women. It was during those years that Munetsura served under Ukita Hideie, who had succeeded his father in 1582, in Toyotomi Hideyoshi's campaign to unify the country, as well as the two Korean campaigns during the nineties.

The Shinmen fortunes again took a turn for the worse in 1600, when Ukita Hideie chose the side of the western forces in the Battle of Sekigahara. Sadly, there are no records on Munetsura's whereabouts during that momentous battle, but like Hideie he lost all of his clan's possessions in its wake.

The next time Munetsura makes his appearance is in records of the Kuroda clan in Chikuzen. Thus, in the *Keichō shichi-nen shoyakunin chigyōwari*, a record of the distribution of land among the the various retainers for the seventh year of Keichō [1602], Munetsura is listed as having a fief of two thousand *koku*. He is also mentioned in the *Keichō nenchū samurai-chū jija chigyō*, a record of the distribution of land among the retainers and the various temples and shrines of the Kuroda clan in Chikuzen from the ninth year of Keichō (1604). Significantly, Munetsura is listed as a newcomer (*shinzan*). In the code of the records this means that Munetsura entered the service of the Koroda sometime after 1600, the year in which the Kuroda moved to their new estate of Chikuzen in reward for their role in the Battle of Sekigahara.

The above, incidentally, also seems to disprove the widely held belief that Musashi's father fought among the western forces (i.e., those of Ukita Hideie) in the battle of Sekigahara under Shinmen Munetsura.

Indeed, it is not even certain whether Munetsura was still in the service of Hideie at that time. The succession from father to son had not gone smoothly. In 1599 a riot had broken out in the Ukita fiefdom, and many of Naoie's close retainers left his son's service and entered the service of Tokugawa Ieyasu, who played an active role in resolving the issue. It is almost certain that at this juncture Munetsura, too, left Hideie's service. He may indeed have gone on to fight under an eastern commander. That would also explain why he was able to enter the service of the Kuroda shortly after the battle. Given that his possessions were part and parcel of the Ukita fief, he would have lost them anyway, regardless of which side he fought for. His fief when he entered the service of the Kuroda, by the way, was only one thousand *koku*, a fifth of what he had owned under Hideie.

- If the *Tōsakushi* is correct Muni was in the service of Shinmen Munetsura at least until 1589, the year in which the latter ordered him to slay his chief deshi, Honiden Gekinosuke. This is supported by other records, in particular the *Shinmen kaki*, and the *Mimasaka taiheiki*, a record of the Kan clan from the Tatsuta district of Mimasaka compiled around the middle of the nineteenth century by a certain Minagi Yasuzane.

The first time Muni makes his entry in the *Mimasaka taiheiki* is in 1583, when it describes how the Shinmen and Yasuhigashi clans joined forces in a night attack on the stronghold of their arch-enemies, the Harada clan:

> When, in the summer of the eleventh year of Tenshō [1583], there was a secret communication from their headquarters in Bizen to both the houses of Shimen and Yasuhigashi to destroy the house of Harada, they rejoiced and secretly sent word to the house of Kanke, and the latter put Yasuhigashi Gensaemon and [Yasuhigashi] Sakon no Suke in charge of a preemptive force of eighty men, including fourteen samurai and fifteen *teppō ashigaru*. And from the house of Shinmen they appointed Uehara Sakon as their spearhead commander, with the two commanders Shinmen Gendayū and Hirata Muni leading thirteen veterans and a force of ninety-four *teppō ashigaru*.

And again in the *Mimasaka taiheiki* for the year 1587:

> In the spring of the fifteenth year of Tenshō, the members of the Shinmen clan, Iguchi Nagabei and Shinmen Shubei fell out with his lordship Iga no Kami [Munetsura] and conspired to rebel against him. They entered in secret negotiations with [the master of] Yahazu castle of Kamogo, and welcomed a large Kusakari force at Heidaka castle in the Ōno

district. The Kusakari assembled a group of seven brave lancers who attacked the castle's wooden gate.

Observing the bravery with which Hirata fought, and realizing moreover that there was none among his retainers who were equal to him in wielding the *yari*, his lordship commended him and gave him the name Hirata Muni [Hirata Who Has no Equal]. And when the enemy ganged in on him, he moved in without boasting, halted their advance, wrested the seven *yari* from their grip and drove them back, killing one and giving chase to the remainder. And this was the technique that Hirata from then on referred to as *shichi-hon-yari*, "the seven lances."

A similar encounter in recounted in the *Shinmen kaki*, the family records of the Shimen clan, which claims that already in the spring of the sixth year of the Tenshō era [1578] Munetsura and his adversary, Kusakari Shigetsugu, met several times in battle after the latter attacked the Shinmen stronghold of Takeyama castle. At a pivotal juncture in of one of those battles:

> Seven warriors among the enemy sought to strike Muni down with their *yari*, but Hirata skillfully took hold of their *yari*, running down as many as three enemy warriors, taking their heads, and giving chase to the remainder, thereby defeating the Kusakari forces.

And again in the *Shinmen kaki*, but this time for the first year of Bunroku (1592):

When Bizen Chūnagon Ukita Hideie laid siege to Hōgan castle of the Kisō clan, Shinmen Iga no Kami [Munetsura] joined forces and made battle, breaching the castle's wall on the south east. Hideie's forces now stormed in, among them Hassha Jūemon, Hirata Muni, Shinmen Higo, and all the Haruna men from the Ohara clan were the first in, taking thirty six heads.

Whilst differently dated, both accounts seem to refer to the same conflict. When corroborated by other sources, the first account seems to be the most accurate, at least where the date of the event is concerned.

What is certain is that Muni had already entered the service of the Kuroda before the turn of the century, i.e., well before his former master Shinmen Munetsura. That much, at least, is borne out by the *Keichō nenchū samurai-chū jija chigyō*. In that document Muni is listed as a *furugo fudai*, or an long-standing hereditary vassal, which, again in the code of the recorder, means that he had entered the service of the Kuroda before 1600, the year in which the Kuroda were promoted to their new estate in Chikuzen. Muni, in other words, entered the service of the Kuroda before the Battle of Sekigahara and not together with Shinmen Munetsura. He can, therefore, not have taken part in that battle under Munetsura as many (including Yoshikawa Eiji) would have us believe.

- The background to the assassination of Honiden is provided by the *Shinmen kaki*, or the *Family Record of the Shinmen Clan*. It describes how, in the autumn of 1588, Shinmen Munetsura invited a company of high-class prostitutes from Kyoto for a tryst.

After a day filled with entertainment, the company spent a night in the field, enjoying a banquet of delicious *matsutake* mushrooms, the gathering of which had occupied much of the day. The *Shinmen kaki* captures the moment in which the innocent Honiden Gekinosuke seals his fate by failing to look away at the right moment when the prostitutes are carried back to Takeyama castle in his lordship's palanquins:

> Honiden Gekinosuke had been visiting Edōji Sanzuke and was just on his way back when he ran into their palanquins as they entered the castle's main gate and, being taken by surprise, he stood and stared as they passed by. One of the women, however, spotted him and asked of her escort Kameemon who it was that was standing and staring at them at the gate's entrance. Kameemon answered saying: "That can be no one else but our samurai Honiden Gekinosuke. A few days later the women spoke to Munetsura and told him that they had been watched by his samurai, which greatly displeased his lordship.

- The gravestone above the old *yashiki* does not mark the grave of Muni (who died in Kyushu), but probably that of his father Buni. The date on the grave, which is today situated on the ground of the Musashi shrine, just south of Miyamoto village, reads "eighteenth day of the fourth month of the eighth year of Tenshō [May 31, 1580]."

❂ Miyamoto Musashi

Miyamoto Musashi's family name is Minamoto (alternatively

Fujiwara). He was Hirata Muni's son. (The *Honchō bugei shoden* and the *Kokura hibun* are wrong in claiming that he hailed from Harima.) His father, Muni, was an adept in the art of swordsmanship and fighting with the *jitte*. When Musashi was still young he observed the shrine officials pounding the great *taikō* drum at the Aramaki shrine. He perceived how the sound from the left and rights side of the drum they produced with their two drum sticks was in perfect unison, and doing away with the *jitte*, he began to practice with two swords on a mallet he had hung up in an empty room of the house.

At the age of twelve he went to Harima and dueled with Arima Kihei and won, and in the province of Tajima he defeated Akiyama in duel. Afterwards, he defeated the Yoshioka in Kyoto and again, on the island of Funashima in the province of Buzen, he met in duel with Sasaki Ganryū and killed him. All in all he engaged in more that sixty duels from the age of twelve and called his school of swordsmanship the Hinoshita Kaizan Shinmei Miyamoto Musashi Seimei-ryū. He distinguished himself on the battlefield during the Battle of Sekigahara and the siege of Osaka castle, and at the time of the Shimabara Rebellion he went into battle under the Hosokawa. He passed away in Kumamoto in the province of Higo on the nineteenth day of the fifth month of the second year of Shōhō [June 13, 1645]. His posthumous name was Genshin Niten.

When Musashi was living in Harima, a practitioner of the martial arts by the name of Musō Gonnosuke came and visited him and desired to duel with him. Musashi was busy crafting a small willow bow. Gonnosuke was wearing a *haori* with the words "Musō Gonnosuke, first and foremost practitioner of the art of *heihō* under the heavens," and was wielding a long *bokutō*. Musashi then stood up and engaged him in a duel with the bow he was holding, but the latter could not find an opening in Musashi's defense.

I believe Musashi had three sons. His oldest son, Iori, was in the service of Lord Hosokawa on a stipend of one thousand *koku*. His second son, Shume, was in the service of the Lord of Kokura, from the house of Ogasawara, and became a chief retainer with a fief of three thousand *koku*. His third son, Mikinosuke, was in fact the son of Shinmen Uemon, and served the Lord of Himeji, from the house of Honda on a stipend of seven hundred *koku*.

Musashi's senior deshi was Takao Magonoshin, his second deshi was Takao Kyūnosuke (who saw action during the Shimabara Rebellion and is listed as a man of many abilities). Furuhashi Sōzaemon, who was a secretary to the house of Hosokawa, exceeded Musashi's other deshi (including Takao Magonosuke and Takao Kyūnosuke) in swordsmanship. He died in Edo.

Musashi had an older sister. Hirata Muni adopted a man by the name of Kinugasa Kurōji, and made him his heir by letting him marry his daughter.

Even today there is a descendant from the house of Miyamoto by the name of Jinemon. Others from the same house, among them a certain Saheiji from the village of Tateishi, and a certain Yoheiji from the village of Shitamachi, are all descendants from the house of Miyamoto.

- Teruo is not the first chronicler to claim that Musashi came from the village of Miyamoto in Yoshino and not Miyamoto village in Harima. That somewhat dubious honor goes to Mikami Genryū, who in his *Gekken sōdan* (1590) states that "Master Musashi was born in the village of Miyamoto in the Yoshino district of Mimasaka province." Teruo, however, does seem to be one of the most ardent proponents of the so-called Mimasaka-*setsu*, or the Mimasaka narrative of Musashi's life. Indeed, he explicitly states that the *Honchō bugei shoden* (1714) is wrong in claiming that Musashi hailed from Harima. In doing so Teruo seems to go against a number of other records on Miyamoto Musashi, many of which were written decades, if not centuries before the *Tōsakushi*. The *Harima kagami* (1762), for instance, states that "Miyamoto Musashi hailed from the village of Miyamoto in the vicinity of Ikaruga in the district of Ittō." Nor does the *Shimoshō mura kojichō* — a record from the village of Shoshō in Mimasaka province — support Teruo's view. More importantly, in his *Gorin no sho*, Musashi was the first to claim that he was a native from Harima.

There may, however, be good reasons why Musashi preferred to consider himself a native of Harima rather than Mimasaka. First of all his father, with whom he had a troubled relationship, came from Mimasaka, whereas his beloved stepmother, Yoshiko, came from Harima. It was at her birthplace, the village of Hirafuku in Harima, that he spent the happiest years of his childhood.

Another reason for Musashi's willing misrepresentation of his roots may be the fact that, like many of the other western provinces, the province of Mimasaka had been the breeding ground of Tokugawa dissent in the run-up to the Battle of Sekigahara. Indeed, Ukita Hideie, at that time the daimyo of both Bizen and Mimasaka, was one of the ringleaders of the Mitsunari alliance and one of the first to mobilize his troops when he held a ceremony for those who would go into battle at the Hōkoku shrine in Fukuoka.

This was on September 8, eleven days before Ishida Mitsunari and his co-conspirators decided to move against Ieyasu at a secret conference at Mitsunari's stronghold of Sawayama castle.

Nor are some of the records that have traditionally been used by proponents of the Harima-*setsu*, or the Harima narrative, as explicit as some historians would suggest. The *Honchō bugei shoden*, for instance, merely states that Musashi "hailed" from the province of Harima and that he was "a scion of the Shinmen, a strand of the Akamatsu." Thus one might consider someone who has been raised in Harima as someone who hails from Harima. Equally, the *Shimoshō mura kojichō* merely states that Musashi "left the country for Kyushu," not specifying whether the country in question (lit. *tōkoku*) was Mimasaka or Harima. Even Musashi's Buddhist friend Akiyama Wanao (1618–73) seems to have shied away from explicitly stating that his friend had been born in Harima. Thus the *Kokura hibun* (1654) only mentions that Musashi was a scion of the Shinmen, last descendants of the Akamatsu of Harima.

Significantly, in his *Tomari jinja munefuda* (1653) Musashi's adopted son Iori states that:

> Among the Akamatsu diaspora of the province of Mimasaka there were those who belonged to a line called the Shinmen. During the Tenshō era [1573–92] the Shinmen line came to an end at Akizuki castle in the province of Chikuzen because there was no successor. Heir to this house and heritage was a man named Musashi Genshin, who later took on the family name of Miyamoto.

- Where most records are content with merely mentioning that Musashi was a scion of the Shinmen, a strand of the Akamatsu, the *Tomari jinja munefuda*—the very first written record of Musashi outside those from his own hand—establishes a clear link between Musashi and the Shinmen from Mimasaka.

    It is here where the *Tōsakushi* and the other records in the Mimasaka-*setsu* tradition become so compelling. They, after all, seek to shed light on Musashi's roots, his youth, and the setting in which he was raised, rather than just dwelling on his later life as a swordsman.

- Teruo seems to mix up Musashi's sons. It was Iori, in fact, who was in the service of the house of Ogasawara and not the house of Hosokawa. He is also the only one to mention that Musashi had a son called Shume, although, if this was the case, he might have been in the service of the Ogasawara, as Teruo claims. He is right, however, in stating that Mikinosuke was in the service of the house of Honda—Honda Tadatoki, to be precise—but wrong in thinking that the boy was a son of Shinmen Uemon. In fact, through the *Hōkōsho* (see the relevant chapter), we now know that Mikinosuke was the third son of Nakagawa Shimanosuke, a descendant of the lord of Nakagawabara castle in the province of Ise.

    If we are to believe the *Hōkōsho*, Mikinosuke had a younger brother by the name of Kurōtarō, who was living with him at the time he served Honda Tadatoki (1569–1626). This would suggest that Musashi not only adopted Mikinosuke after the siege of Osaka castle, but also his younger brother. No other record makes any mention of Kurōtarō, and it is possible that Mikinosuke took his younger brother under his care on his own account after he entered Tadatoki's service sometime after 1617 (the year in which Tadatoki was promoted to his new fief of Nitta in Harima).

In he absence of any such evidence, it is hard to believe that Teruo is referring to Mikinosuke's younger brother when he is talking of Shume.

- Teruo was probably also wrong in claiming Musashi had an older sister. This error was the result of one of the records the historian consulted in his research, specifically, a misreading of the *Shimoshō mura kojichō-yo*, or *Copy of the Old Records of the Village of Shimoshō*, which was written in 1689 and is now in the possession of the local Hirao clan. The misreading concerns the confusion of the characters for sister and daughter. Though the two have the same radical, *jō*, and look very similar, the original *Shimoshō mura kojichō* clearly mentions that Miyamoto Kurōtarō's wife was Muni's younger sister (*imōto*), and not his daughter (*musume*). If the rest of the *Tōsakushi* is to be believed, then, Miyamoto Kurōjirō married Musashi's aunt and had a son called Yōemon.

- Teruo's claim that Musashi took part in the suppression of the Shimabara Rebellion under the command of the Hosokawa is also incorrect. Musashi was assigned as an escort to Ogasawara Nagatsugu, the young son of Ogasawara Tadazane, the lord of Musashi's second adopted son, Iori.

❦ Musashi's *bokutō*

Among Miyamoto Musashi Seimei's personal possessions in the collection of Moriiwa Nagataifu was a *bokutō*. Its length was six *shaku*, four *bu*, and five *ri* [approx. three-and-a-half feet]. Its thickness at the hilt was four *bu* and five *rin* [approx. one-half inch], and at the tip two *bu* and five *rin* [approx. one-quarter inch]. Along its center ran an edge, causing the weapon's thickness at the middle to swell to five *bu*, while its upper and lower edge was rounded along the entire length. It was made of a loquat tree, its color being black and having an exceedingly old and stained look.

According to legend Moriiwa Hikobei would accompany Miyamoto Musashi to the Kamazaka hills of Nakamura whenever he went on one of his *musha shugyō*. At such times he would give Hikobei his walking cane and they would say their farewells. In fact, he finally gave Hikobei his *bokken*. Moriiwa Nagataifu also had among his collection a small statue of Kannon to whom Musashi would pray, but it has recently been lost. It is said that the house of Moriiwa is a very old one.

- Next to nothing is known of Moriiwa Hikobei, but a stone monument dedicated to his memory can still be found near the Musashi shrine on the outskirts of Musashi village.

Musashi's descendants

Among the rural dwellings of this village there is an old building that marks the place of Musashi's old *yashiki*. It seemed to have occupied some three thousand square yards, and to have been the place where Miyamoto Muni dwelled long ago. It is said that at the time of the Shimabara Rebellion, the stone wall that surrounded it was demolished by order of the authorities.

Since Muni's descendants still live in the said village, I will write down their names:

> Miyamoto Muni, and his son Miyamoto Musashi;
> Miyamoto Kurōjirō's wife and Muni's daughter,
> and Kurōjirō's son Miyamoto Yōemon;

Miyamoto Yōemon's son Miyamoto Kurōemon,
and Kurōemon's son Miyamoto Shichirōemon;
Shichirōemon's son Miyamoto Shichirōemon,
and Shichirōemon's deshi Niemon.

Muni's son Musashi lived here sometime between the Tenshō [1573–93] and the Keichō [1596–1616] eras. After that, in the ninth year of Genna [1623], Musashi's descendants moved to the rice fields above the old building (as seen from the village of Shimoshō) and continued the house of Musashi from Yōemon onward.

Miyamoto Musashi left the said village ninety years ago. At the time, he gave the household tools, family lineage, and his deed into the custody of Yōemon. Afterwards, they were passed on to Kurōemon, who moved down to a place less than a mile from the village of Miyamoto, where he took up life as a farmer.

According to yet another document Musashi left his household tools, his *jitte*, three chains, *yari*, and his clan's lineage in the possession of Yōemon when he set out on his travels, but that they were destroyed in a fire at the time of Kurōemon some sixty years ago.

One can see the words "Shinmen tributary branch of the Akamatsu" on Musashi's monument epitaph, and in certain records a link is made to the Hirao clan, and again, when looking at the family lineage of the Hirata clan, Musashi's family lineage is as written below, although I am not sure which of them is correct:

Hirata Shōkan - Hirata Muni - Hirata Musashi
- Hirata Busuke - Hirata Jirōsaemon
- Hirata Jirōdayū

- Teruo seems to have taken his cue from the *Shimoshō mura kojichō* where it concerned the fate of Musashi's earthly possessions after he departed for Kyushu. Indeed, his text is almost identical to that of the old village records, which claims that, "Ninety years ago Miyamoto Musashi left the country for Kyushu. At the time, he gave the household tools, family lineage, and his deed into the custody of Yōemon. Afterwards, they were passed on to Kurōemon, who moved down to a place less than a mile from the village of Miyamoto, where he took up life as a farmer. The said items were destroyed in a fire sixty years ago."

❂ The *Mimasaka ryakushi* ⁽¹⁸⁸¹⁾

Like the *Tōsakushi*, the *Mimasaka ryakushi* is closely connected to the Tsuyama fief in the province of Mimasaka. Issued in 1881, the *Mimasaka ryakushi* is a historical record of the old province of Mimasaka (part of today's Okayama prefecture), from ancient times to the end of the Tokugawa Bakufu. It was recorded by Yabuki Masanori (1833–1906), a retainer of Matsudaira Naritami (1814–191), the then daimyo of the Tsuyama fief and the master of Tsuyama castle.

A native of Mimasaka, Masanori was trained in history as well as the art of gunnery. During the Mitō Rebellion (1864–65) he mediated on behalf of his lord, who supported the court against the waning influence of the Tokugawa Bakufu. Following the rebellion's repression by Bakufu troops Masanori was temporarily placed under house arrest.

In the wake of the Meiji Restoration, Masanori was acquitted and raised to the rank of senor retainer. In 1871, following the dismantling of the fief system, he became an official at the government organ in Tsuyama that ran the newly established Hokujō prefecture (formerly Mimasaka, but now part of Okayama). In 1876, he retired and became the chief editor of Tsuyama's town gazette and a shrine official at the town's ancient Nakayama shrine. Masanori spent much of his free time writing and editing local histories on Tsuyama, the Mori, and Matsudaira clans, and many of the local shrines. Yet he is perhaps best known for his comprehensive history of the province of Mimasaka, the *Mimasaka ryakushi*, which comprises four volumes.

Masanori is one of the few historians to actually refer to the records he consulted in order to derive at his reconstruction of Musashi's life. Thus we know that he relied on works such as the *Honchō buigei shoden* and the *Gekken sōdan*. Another important work to play an important role in Masanori's reconstruction is referred to as a "detailed account from the Genroku era." The account in question is a short work called the *Shimoshō mura kojichō*, a record from a village in Mimasaka province from which the author of the *Tōsakushi* also drew information.

❧ Miyamoto Seimei

In the fifth year of Keichō [1600], a man from the Yoshino district by the name of Miyamoto Semei went to Kyushu (according to the [*Honchō*] *bugei shoden*, the *Gekken sōdan* and a detailed record from the Genroku era). Seimei was [also] called Miyamoto (the *Gekken sōdan* speaks of Yoshitsune). He hailed from the village of Miyamoto (in the district of Yoshino). His ancestors belonged to the Kinugasa, a clan descendant from the Akamatsu. They lived in the village of Hirao in Harima and took their clan's name from the village. When Seimei was alive he took the name of the village of Miyamoto and made it his clan's name. His father, Tarōemon, was a retainer of Shinmen Munetsura, and was renowned for his skill with the *jitte*, and known under the name of Shinmen Munisai.

From a young age Seimei pursued his father's art of combat, as well as excelling in the field of painting. When he came of age twelve he first began to dedicate himself to the art of swordsmanship, which he studied in Harima. When he completed his study he traveled around the country, meeting famed *bushi*, competing with them in skill as many as sixty times, yet without having ever been defeated once. The people at the time called this, "without equal in Japan." He will be remembered by future generations for his victory over Yoshioka Kenpō in Kyoto and his slaying of Sasaki Ganryū on the island of Funashima.

In this year of Keichō the Ukita clan were annihilated and Shinmen Munetsura entered the service of Kuroda Nagamasa. Seimei, too, left the province and traveled down to Kyushu. In the second year of Shōhō [1645] Seimei passed away in Kumamoto in the province of Higo. At the time his son Iori was in the service of the Ogasawara clan, who were the masters of Kokura castle, and he was counted among their senior retainers.

- Masanori's claim that Musashi left for Kyushu in 1600 is not supported by the works he refers to. Neither the *Honchō bugei shoden* nor the *Gekken sōdan* make mention of Musashi leaving for Kyushu. It is supported, however, by the *Shimoshō mura kojichō-yo*, a *Copy of the Old Records of the Village of Shimoshō*, written in 1689 (also see the notes to the chapter on the *Tōsakushi*), which claims that Musashi "left the country for Kyushu ninety years ago," (not specifying, by the way, which country it is referring to). Given that the record in question was written in the second year of Genroku (1689), it would mean that Musashi left (Mimasaka?) in 1599, not in 1600.
- Masanori clearly takes his cue from the *Honchō bugei shoden* where it comes to Musashi's name. That record, after all, is the first one to erroneously claim that the swordsman's full name was Miyamoto Musashi Seimei. This, again, is to ignore far more reliable sources, beginning with the swordsman himself, who, in the opening paragraph of his *Gorin no sho*, clearly states, "My name is Shinmen Musashi no Kami

Fujiwara no Genshin." The *Kokura hibun*, too, speaks of Shinmen Musashi Genshin. Likewise, Hayashi Razan dedicates his tribute to "Shinmen Genshin," while Musashi's adopted son Iori speaks of "Musashi Genshin, who later took on the family name of Miyamoto," when referring to his adoptive father in the *Tomari jinja munefuda*.

- The *Mimasaka ryakushi* is the only record to mention the reason Shinmen Munetsura entered the service of the Kuroda, i.e., the annihilation of the Ukita clan. In the Battle of Sekigahara, Ukita Hideie chose the side of the western alliance under Ishida Mitsunari. Defeated in battle he fled to the Ibuki Mountains, from where, with the help of Shimazu Yoshihiro (1535–1619) of Satsuma, he made his way in disguise to the province of Ōsumi (today's Kagoshima prefecture). Equally deprived of his former possessions (but not necessarily because he fought under Ukita during the same battle), Shinmen Munetsura entered the service of Kuroda Yoshitaka sometime after 1600, the year in which the latter was promoted to his new estate in Chikuzen in reward for his role in the Battle of Sekigahara (also see the notes to the *Tōsakushi*).

- The Mitō Rebellion (also Kantō or Tengutō Rebellion) was a local uprising against the power of the Bakufu, who in the eyes of the rebels were too accomodating of the interference in Japanese affairs by foreign powers. Their solution was expressed in the slogan *Sonnō, jō-i*, i.e, "Revere the Emperor, expel the barbarians."

The *Bisan hōkan* (1897)

Ironically, while the latest of records on Musashi featured here, the *Bisan hōkan* is at the same time the most obscure. A collection of anecdotes about persons, places, and events from the provinces of Owari and Mikawa, it is one of the few records to relate Musashi's experiences in Himeji when he was probably living in nearby Hirafuku with his mother and newly adopted son Mikinosuke in the wake of the siege of Osaka castle. The *Bisan hōkan* was compiled in 1897 by three historians, Kosuge Ren, Itō Kōnosuke, and Kasahara Kubo.

Where next to nothing is known about its authors, the *Bisan hōkan* is very clear about its ambitions. Issued in 1897, in the wake of the (first) Sino-Japanese War (1894–95), the *Bisan hōkan* is already infused with the nationalist fervor that swept the country following the resounding victory over a rival in whose cultural shadow it had — at least in the Nationalist's view — been languishing for too long.

Writing in his foreword about the purpose of their work, the group's general editor, Kosuge Ren, is clearly not immune to the prevailing sentiment of the time:

> Since the people of this rising empire are led by patriotism and so guided in their sense of duty, the traditions and customs of the districts and villages of Owari and Mikawa over the last three-hundred-year reign of peace and prosperity recorded in this study have therefore brought forth an abundance of illustrious persons whose works are unequalled in the whole nation.

It was with such lofty ideas in mind that:

> In the nineteenth year of Meiji [1886], we the editors took up the plan to travel the interior in an effort to collect historical anecdotes from all villages and districts and were able to collect some five hundred items.

Luckily, the passage on Musashi is pleasantly devoid of any such patriotic fervor, concentrating instead on an interesting episode during Musashi's time as an instructor to Honda Tadamasa's retainers in Himeji.

It seems odd that a work focusing on the provinces of Owari and Mikawa, separated from Harima by at least four provinces, should be knowledgeable (and indeed concerned) about events in Himeji, were it not for the fact that the house of Honda, which had been the masters of the Himeji fiefdom in Musashi's day, eventually (1769) settled in the fief of Okazaki, which *was* situated in the province of Mikawa, and of which they remained masters until the abolition of the system of fiefdom in 1871.

Along with histories of their rule of many other fiefdoms (which included Kōriyama in Yamato, Yamazaki in Harima, Murakami in Echigo, Koga in Shimōsa, and Hamada in Iwami) the house of Honda brought with them to Okazaki the proud memories of their time in the great castle town of Himeji. And thus, more than two centuries later, the compilers of the *Bisan hōkan* unearthed an episode in Musashi's life that is missing from many other sources.

❧ Musashi and Miyake Gundayū

The Honda of Okazaki became the masters of Himeji, a fief of one-hundred-and-fifty thousand *koku* in Harima. Now the house of Honda prided itself on being the Tokugawa's chief repository of the martial arts. At the time of Tadakatsu's son, Tadamasa, Miyamoto Musashi visited Himeji and opened a *kenjutsu dōjō*, putting up a signpost with the text "Miyamoto Musashi, Japan's Foremost Master of Swordsmanship." When the Himeji retainers heard this they were angered and said, "To come to the castle town of the house of Honda, first among the Four Warrior Demigods, and open a *dōjō* with a signpost proclaiming one is the greatest swordsman in the realm is an outrage." Before long the town grew clamorous, and some voices even went up demanding that he should be killed.

When Honda Tadamasa heard this he said, "If Musashi really is the greatest swordsman in the realm, I would want to make him one of my retainers. If he is not, the shame of defeat in duel will make him leave on his own accord. At this he summoned Himeji's chief swordsman, Miyake Gundayū, and instructed him to put Musashi's martial skills to the test.

Miyake sought out Musashi and presented him with his name card. Musashi let him into his guest room and let him wait for an hour. Miyake thought it below his standing as a commander of a garrison of *ashigaru* that he should be kept waiting. Moreover, since Musashi was no more than a wandering swordsman, it was rude to remain so aloof toward a man of his stature.

Another hour passed and still Musashi would not meet Miyake in person. Now Miyake began to suspect Musashi had read his visiting card and grown fearful and did not want to meet him. Still Musashi did not show his face and before long five hours elapsed. Yet when Miyake furtively looked into the room where

Musashi was staying he found that he was playing a game of *go* at leisure. At length Miyake lost his composure and calling the page, demanded a meeting with Musashi.

Aware that Miyake's anger had reached its boiling point, Musashi made a dignified appearance when he entered the guest room. He apologized for keeping his guest waiting and asked of Miyake what had brought him to his house. At this Miyake proposed that they duel to test Musashi's ability with the sword. Musashi laughed and said, "If I had known that is what you have come for I would not have kept you waiting." Instead I was killing time by playing a game of *go* with another guest. Let us go into the garden. And, come to speak of it, what weapon would you like to use, a sword, or a *bokutō*? I will leave it to you, my honored guest, to decide."

Miyake now grew even more angry. After all, it had been his lordship's wish that he submit Musashi to a test, merely to ascertain his level of skill. He had certainly not come to fight a life and death duel. Not wanting to use a real sword, he cut himself a piece of bamboo from the garden so as to use it as a makeshift *bokutō*. Musashi wielded a *bokutō* as they faced off in the garden. However, Miyake was no match for him and dropped his head in defeat. Thus he returned to Lord Honda Tadamasa, reporting that Musashi's boastful claim that he was the greatest swordsman in the realm was only rightful.

Tadamasa now summoned Musashi and proposed that Musashi enter his service. Musashi, however, declined, saying, "I am an ambitious man, but I do not wish to become a retainer." In the end, Lord Tadamasa granted Musashi a stipend of two hundred *koku* and made him instruct his young clansmen. They flocked to Musashi's gate and studied his art of swordsmanship. As a result, the fame of Miyake's Tōgun-ryū faded and Musashi's Enmei-ryū became the fief's official school of swordsmanship. For two years, Musashi remained at Himeji and his deshi greatly advanced their skills.

When Musashi left Himeji, Miyake Gundayū led his *ashigaru* and ambushed Musashi at Matsubara. Worse still, Miyake's men had not only brought along swords and spears, but were armed with rifles. When they had encircled Musashi and were about to shoot, Musashi dropped his head deeply and apologized. When Miyake saw this he ordered his men to withdraw, at which point Musashi opened his folding fan, wrote down a poem, and handing the closed fan to Miyake, said: "Don't open the fan until you return home. It is my written apology." When Miyake finally opened the fan it read:

> In a world without
> bows and rifles
> Who would win out
> over my art of *heihō*

Enraged Miyake said, "The bastard insulted me!" Yet at the same time he was full of praise, saying, "I'm only good at one thing. But I can't hold a candle to the calligraphy, skill, and martial arts of this man Musashi."

- The bout with Miyake Gundayū is the only recorded match during Musashi's brief stay at Himeji (though he

probably spent much of his time in Hirafuku with his mother and his first adopted son, Mikinosuke).
- The Tōgun-ryū was founded by Kawasaki Kaginosuke, the son of Kawasaki Tokisada, who had been in the service of the illustrious Asakura. At a young age Kaginosuke studied the art of swordsmanship under none other than Toda Seigen, chief propagator of the Toda-ryū, the official school of swordsmanship of the Asakura clan. Following the demise of the Asakura, Kaginosuke led the life of a *rōnin*, until he was taken in by Tōgun Sōjō, abbot of the Hiezan monastery near Kyoto. Kaginosuke continued his study of the art of swordsmanship under Sōjō, naming his school after the Hiezan monk.
- Interestingly, the *Nihon kendō-shi*, published in 1925, features a meeting between Musashi and a man by the name of Miyake Gunbei, followed by a match in the garden of Musashi's dwelling. It describes how Gunbei opens the attack and Musashi gradually retreats until:

> Musashi had his back against the entrance, with no more room to back away. Convinced he had Musashi cornered Gunbei now lowered his *bokutō* and drew the weapon back to run him through the third time round, when Musashi shouted, "Look out," and stabbed him in the face with his short *bokutō*. Gunbei's jaw dropped as fresh blood gushed forward from the wound inflicted by the vigor of his own thrust. Musashi laughed and held back saying, "First wipe this blood away."

Old Provinces

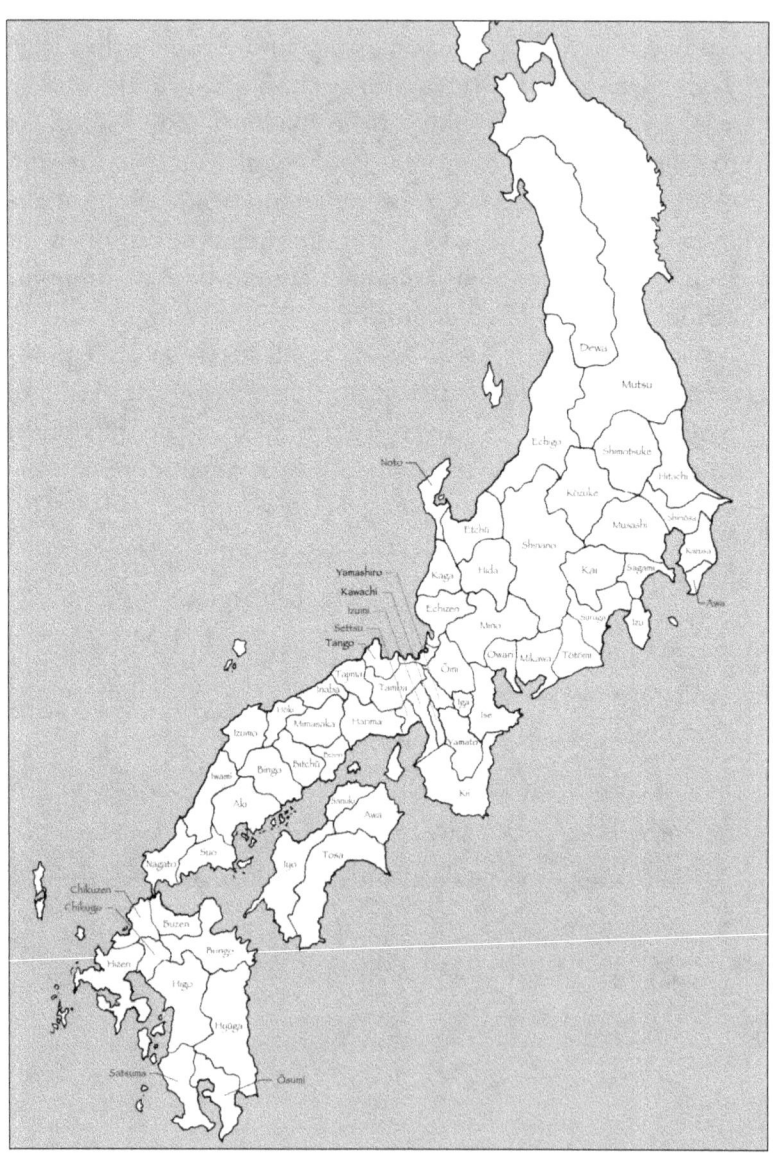

❧ Old Provinces and Their Modern Equivalents

Aki:	Hiroshima	Kazusa:	Chiba
Awa:	Tokushima	Kii:	Wakayama
Bingo:	Hiroshima	Kōzuke:	Gunma
Bitchū:	Okayama	Mikawa:	Aichi
Bizen:	Okayama	Mimasaka:	Okayama
Bungo:	Ōita	Mino:	Gifu
Buzen:	Fukuoka	Musashi:	Saitama and Tokyo
Chikugo:	Fukuoka	Mutsu:	Aomori
Chikuzen:	Fukuoka	Nagato:	Yamaguchi
Dewa:	Yamagata, Akita	Noto:	Ishikawa
Echigo:	Niigata	Ōmi:	Shiga
Echizen:	Fukui	Ōsumi:	Kagoshima
Etchū:	Fukuyama	Owari:	Aichi
Harima:	Hyōgo	Sagami:	Kanagawa
Hida:	Gifu	Sanuki:	Kagawa
Higo:	Kumamoto	Satsuma:	Kagoshima
Hitachi:	Ibaraki	Settsu:	Osaka
Hizen:	Nagasaki	Shimōsa:	Chiba
Hōki:	Tottori	Shinano:	Nagano
Hyūga:	Miyazaki	Suō:	Yamaguchi
Iga:	Mie	Suruga:	Shizuoka
Inaba:	Tottori	Tajima:	Hyōgo
Ise:	Mie	Tamba:	Kyoto
Iwami:	Shimane	Tango:	Kyoto
Iyo:	Ehime	Tosa:	Kōchi
Izu:	Shizuoka	Tōtōmi:	Shizuoka
Izumi:	Osaka	Wakasa:	Fukui
Izumo:	Shimane	Yamashiro:	Kyoto
Kaga:	Ishikawa	Yamato:	Nara
Kai:	Yamanashi		
Kawachi:	Osaka		

Castles, Temples, and Shrines

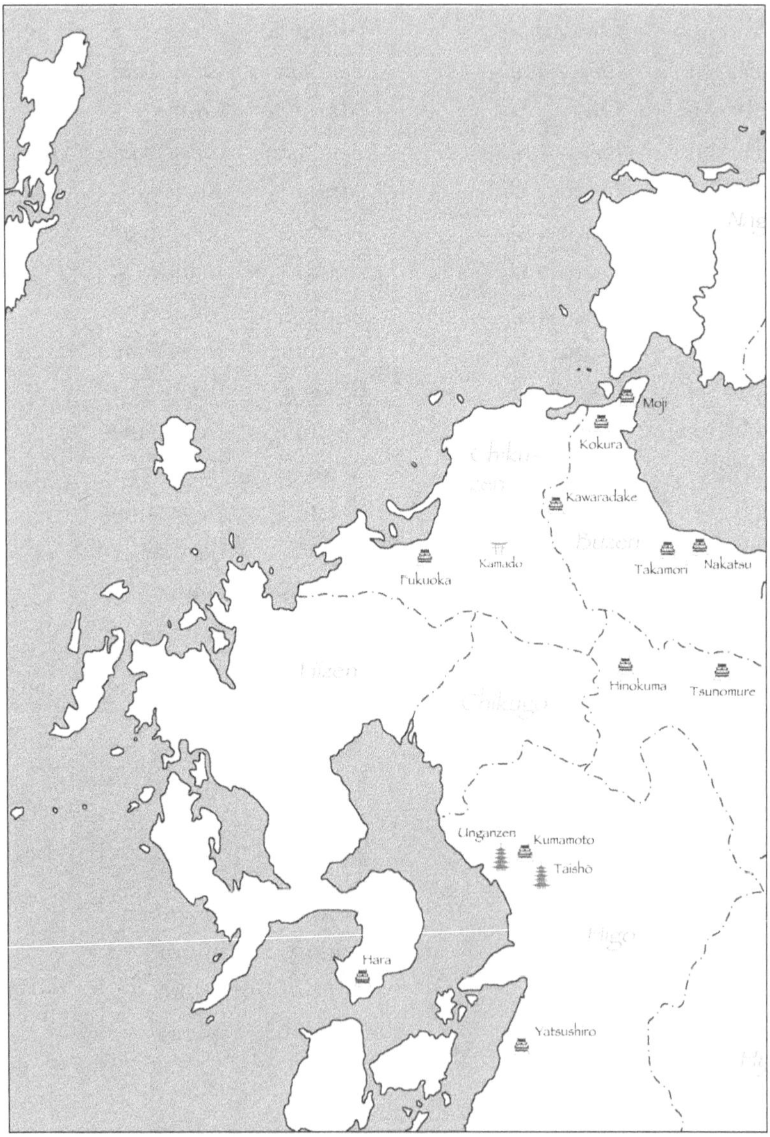

Castles, Temples, and Shrines ● 133

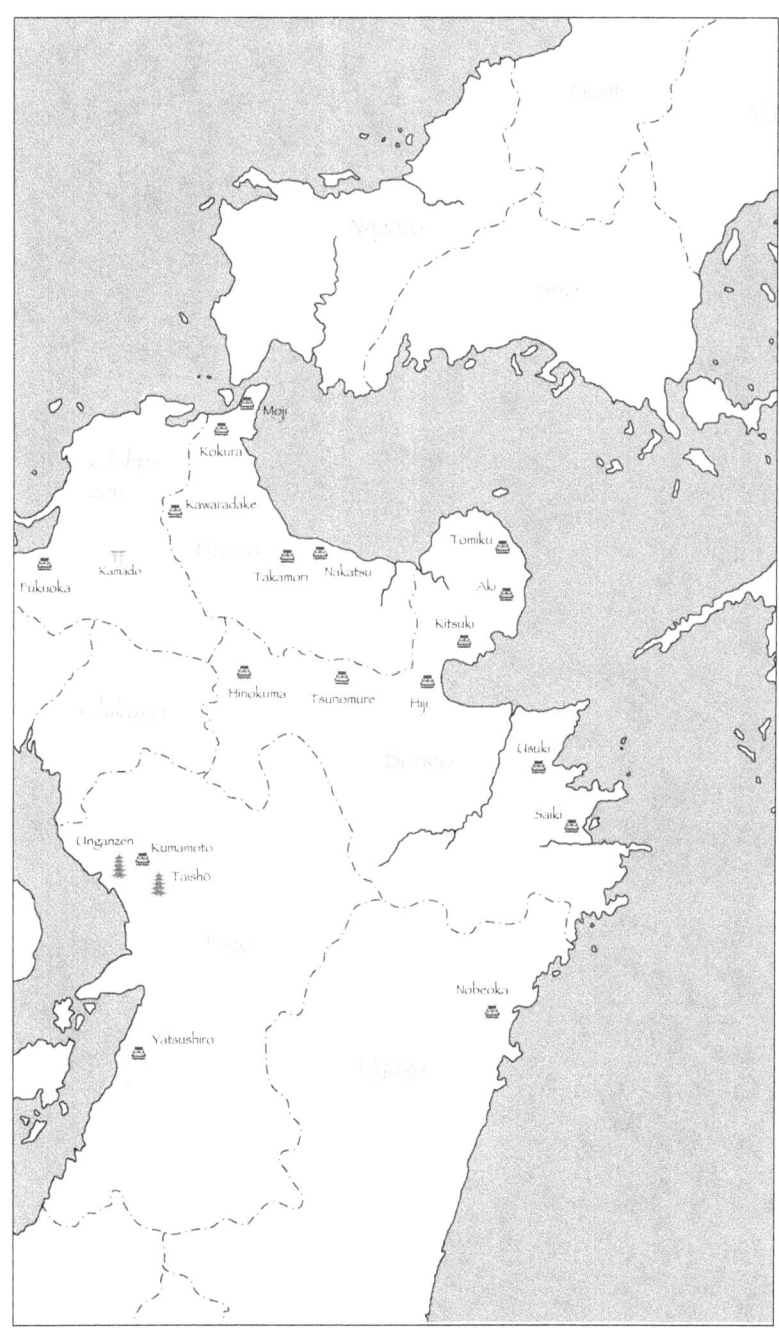

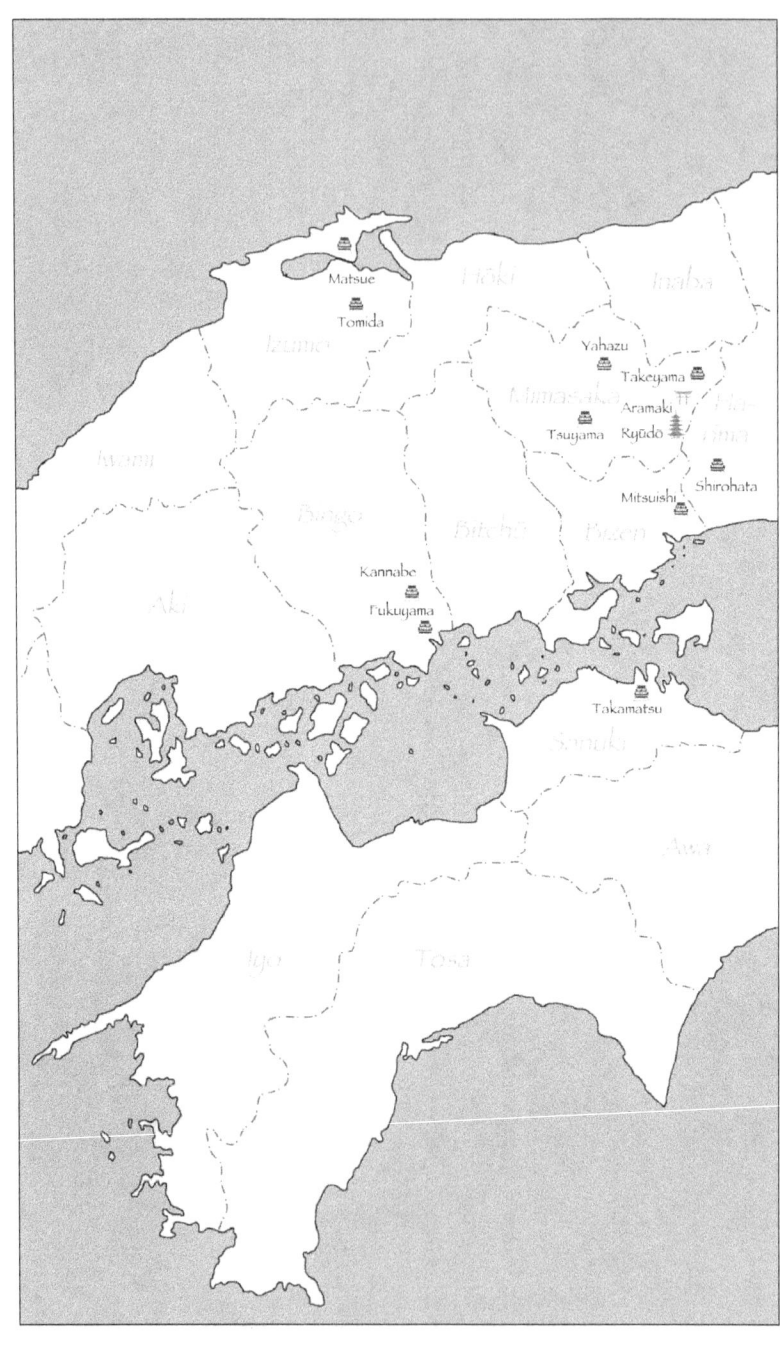

Castles, Temples, and Shrines ❧ 135

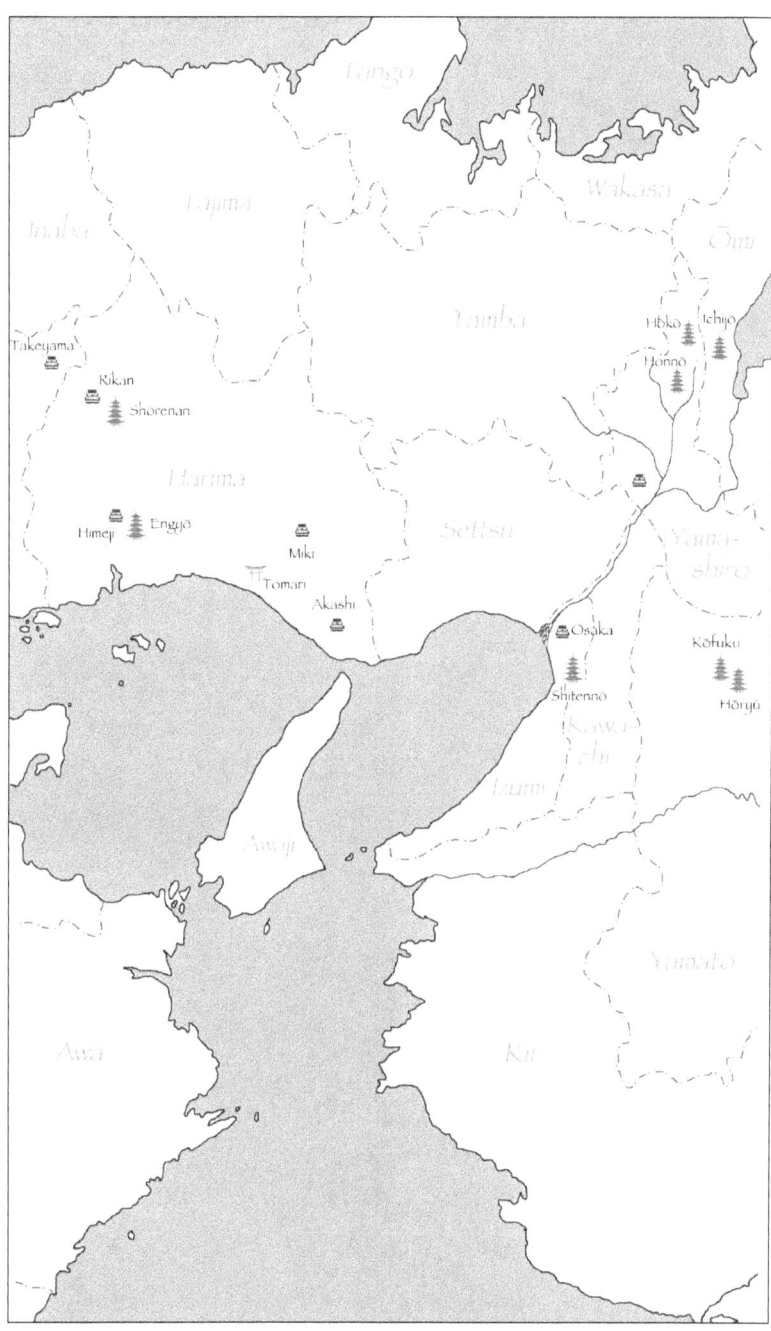

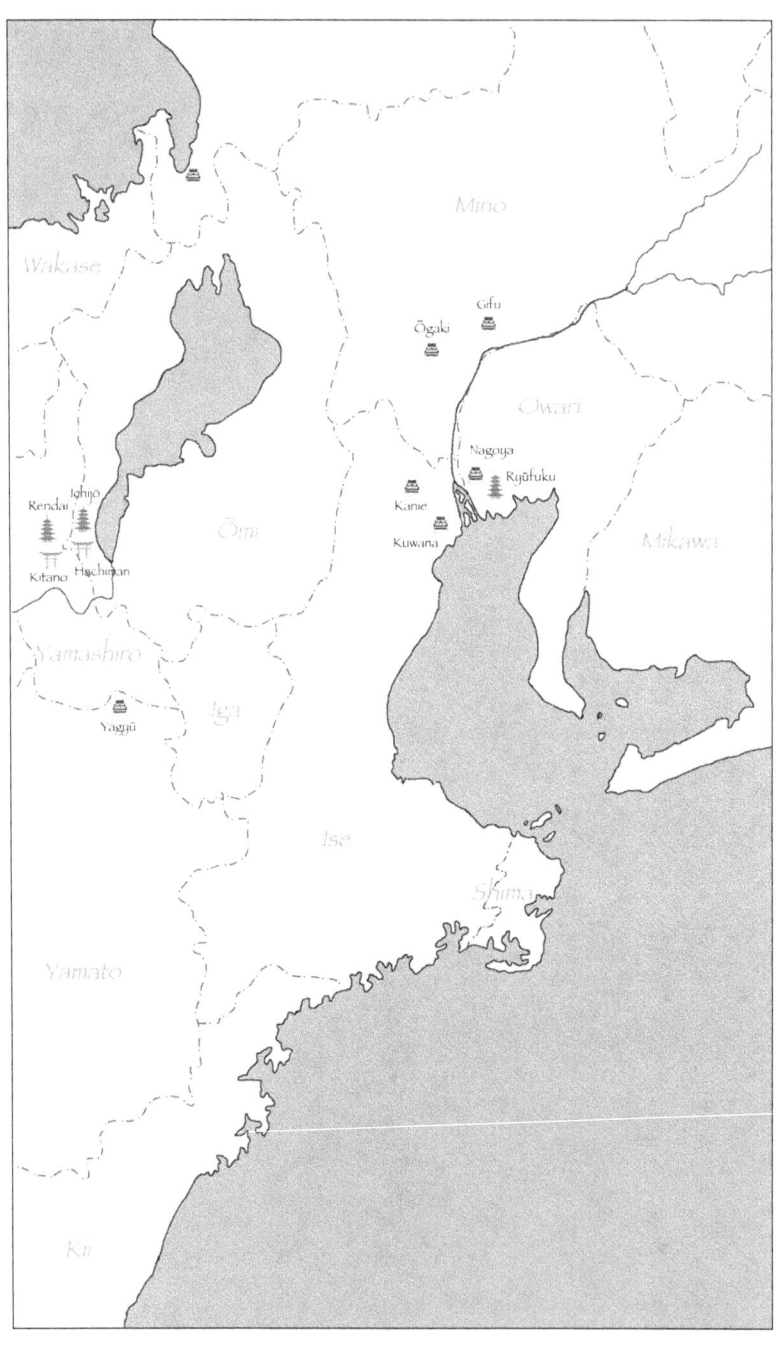

Castles, Temples, and Shrines 137

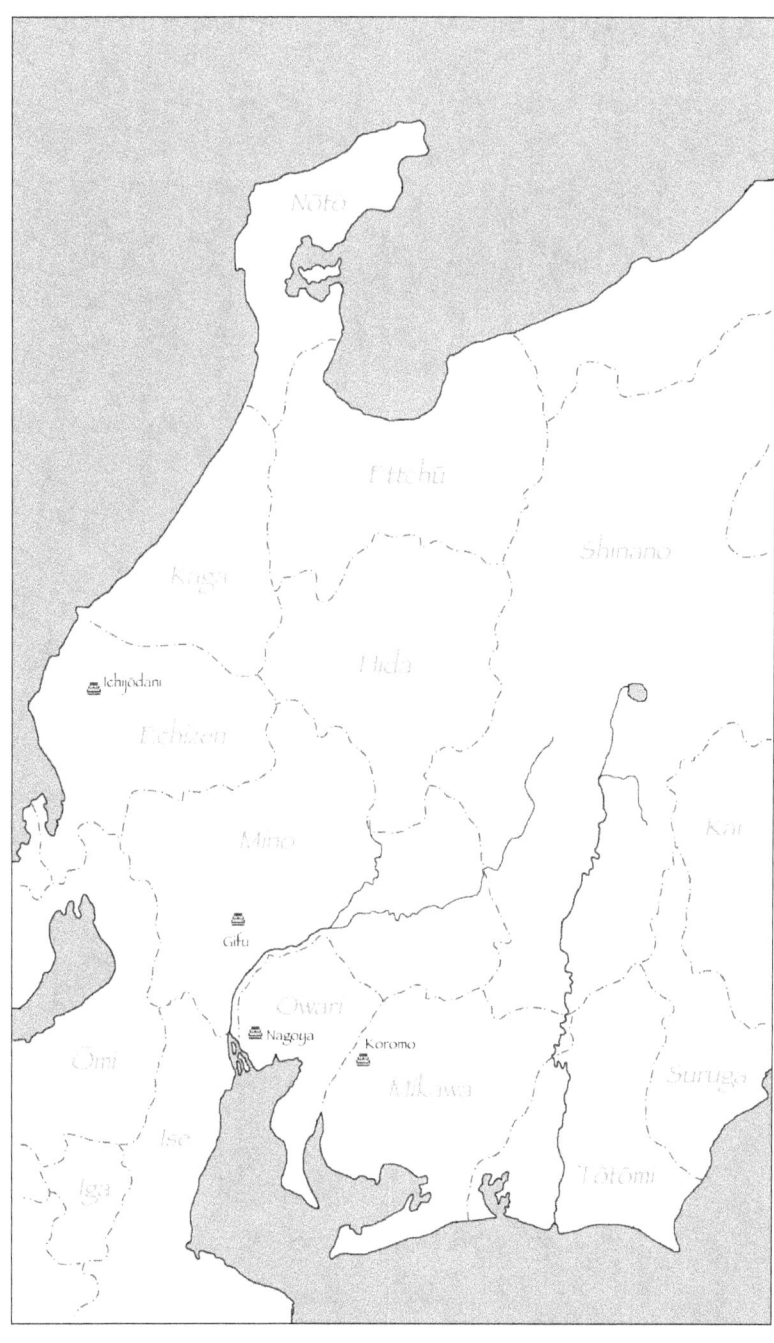

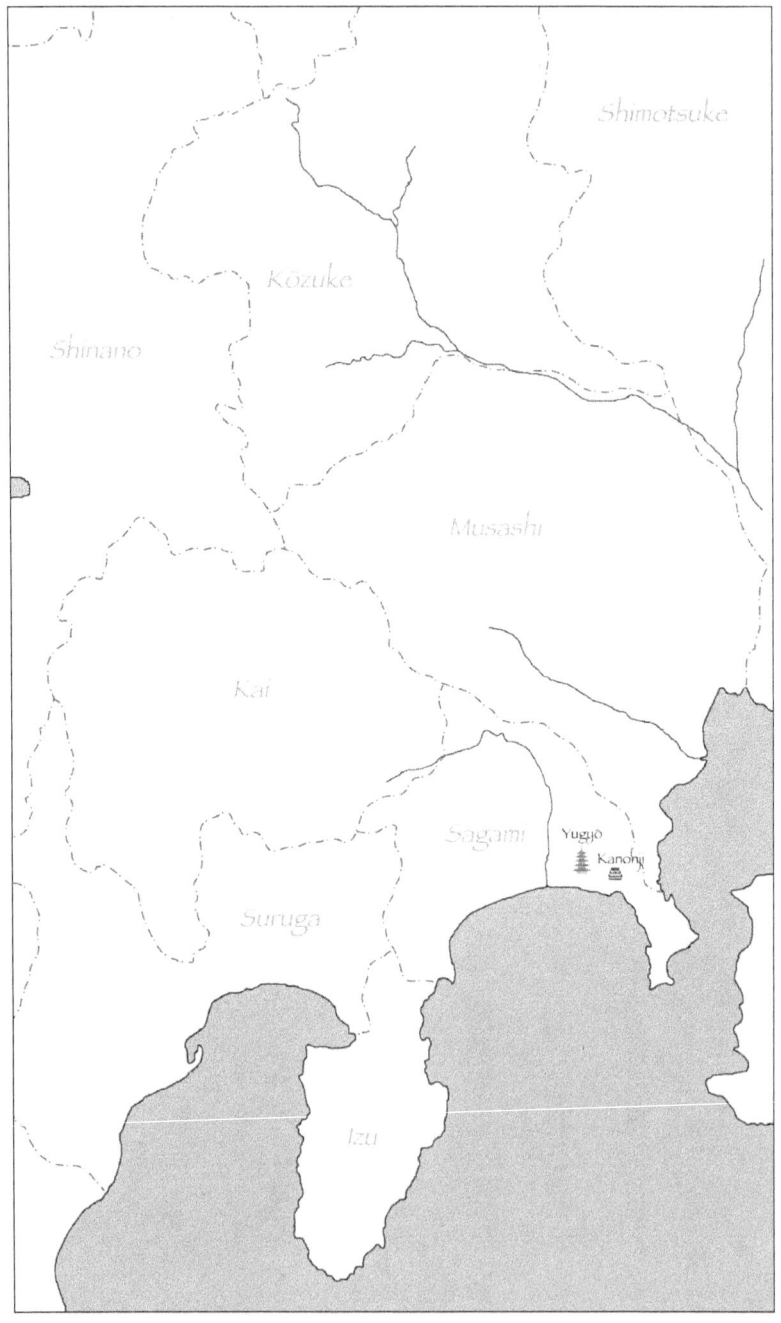

Castles, Temples, and Shrines ❂ 139

140 • The Real Musashi

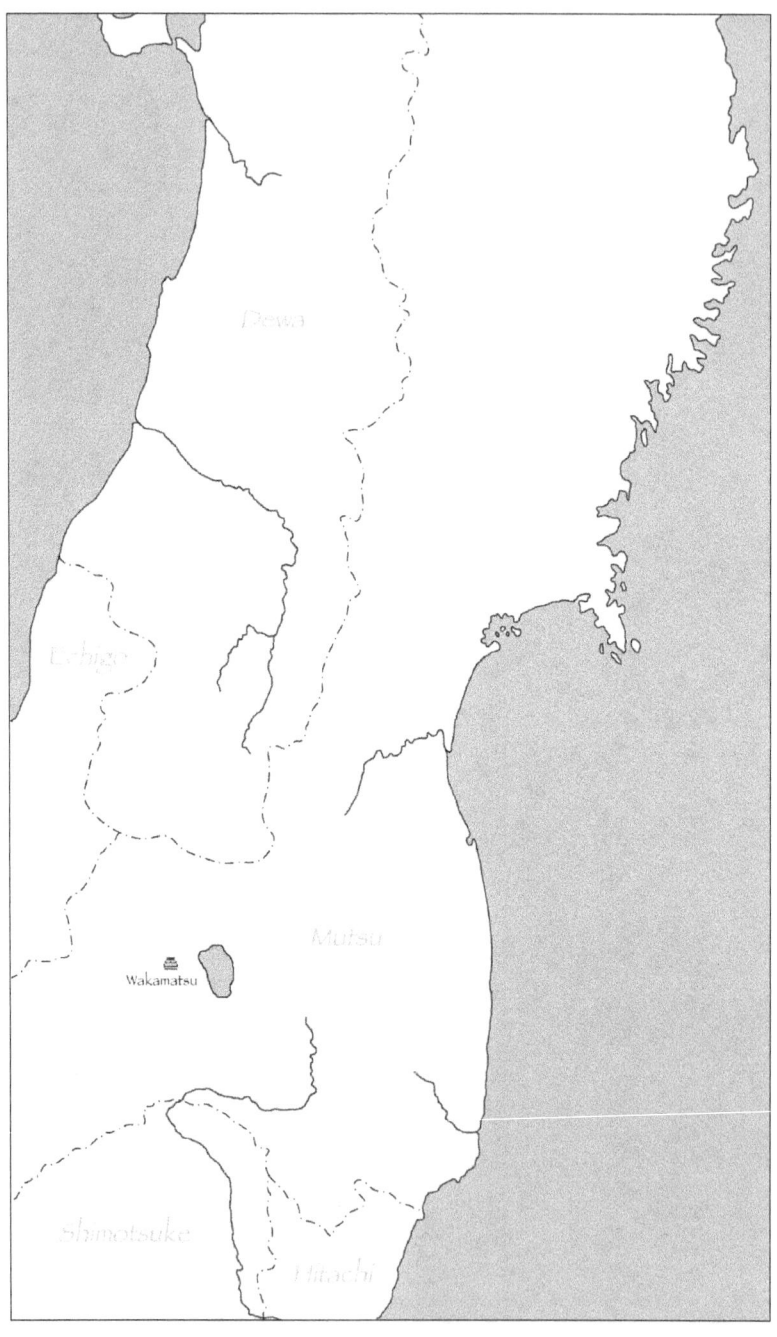

☯ Important Castles

Akashi castle: Headquarters of Ogasawara Tadazane, who hired Musashi as an adviser during its construction.

Aki castle: One of the many castles subdued by Kuroda Yoshitaka during his campaign against the forces of Ōtomo Yoshimune.

Akizuki castle: Castle in Chikuzen where, according to the *Tomari Jinja munefuda*, the Shinmen line came to an end.

Fukuoka castle: Headquarters of the Kuroda clan during the second half of Musashi's life. It was under the control of Kuroda Tadayuki by the time Musashi went into retirement.

Hara castle: Center of the Shimabara Rebellion in which Musashi saw action as the guardian of Ogasawara Nagatsugu.

Himeji castle: Headquarters of Honda Tadamasa and his son, Tadatoki, master of Musashi's first adopted son, Mikinosuke.

Hōgan castle: Headquarters of the Kiso clan.

Kokura castle: Initially the headquarters of Hosokawa Tadatoki, but following his promotion to Kumamoto castle, the seat of the Ogasawara clan, during whose reign Musashi often visited the castle.

Kumamoto castle: Headquarters of the Hosokawa Tadatoshi, the man who allowed Musashi to retire to what had once been the residential quarters of the local Ideta clan.

Miki castle: Besshō Nagaharu's headquarters, some thirty miles south east from Hirafuku.

Moji castle:	Headquarters of Hosokawa Tadatoshi during Musashi's legendary duel with Sasaki Kojirō on Ganryū Island.
Ohara castle:	Castle in Aizu and headquarters of Iori's grandfather, Ohara Nobutoshi.
Osaka castle:	Headquarters of the Toyotomi faction and scene of the summer campaign of 1615 in which Musashi participated under Mizuno Katsunari.
Takeyama castle:	Headquarters of Shinmen Munetsura when Musashi was growing up.
Yahazu castle:	Headquarters of the Kusakari clan.
Yatsushiro castle:	Headquarters of Nagaoka Okinaga, who prevailed on Musashi to leave the Reigan Cave and spend his last days at what had once been the quarters of the local Ideta clan.

Important Temples

Hōkō temple:	Situated in Kyoto and the place where Yoshioka Kenpō got embroiled in a fight and was killed by the assembled guards.
Hoyō temple:	Nichiren temple in Miki village, known for its stone monument for Iori's brother, Genshō.
Ichijō temple:	Situated east of Kyoto and the place where Musashi is believed to have duelled with members of the Yoshioka clan.
Kurama temple:	Temple in Kyoto associated with the Kyōhachi-ryū.
Rendai temple:	Situated in Kyoto and according to Hōkin the place where Musashi duelled with Yoshioka Seijūrō.
Ryūdō temple:	Miyamoto family temple in Musashi's hometown of Miyamoto.
Taishō temple:	The Hosokawa family temple in Kumamoto, led by Akiyama Wanao, one of Musashi close friends in old age.
Yōjū temple:	Situated just south of Kumamoto castle, on the northern bank of the Shira river and once the location of Musashi's mortuary tablet (which was later moved to the grounds of the Taigan temple, where it was destroyed by fire as a result of Allied bombings).

Important Shrines

Arakami shrine: Shrine in Musashi's hometown of Miyamoto, where, according to the *Tōsakushi*, Musashi was inspired to use both swords simultaneously in combat when observing the shrine officials pounding the shrine's great *taikō* drum using two drumsticks.

Hachidai shrine: One of the possible shrines Musashi passed on his way to his duel with Yoshioka Matashichirō, it is situated only a few hundred meters away from the Ichijō temple.

Kitano Hachiman: One of the possible shrines Musashi passed on his way to his duel with Yoshioka Mataschichirō, it is situated west of Kyoto, and equally near an area of the city that is still called Kudarimatsu.

Tomari shrine: Shrine in Iori's hometown of Yoneda and repository of the *Tomari Jinja munefuda*, one of the earliest extant records to mention Musashi.

Historical Periods

Japan

Nara	710–94
Heian	794–1185
Kamakura	1185–1333
Muromachi	1333–1568
Momoyama	1568–1600
Tokugawa	1600–1868

China

Han	202 BC–AD 220
Three Kingdoms	221–65
Six Dynasties	265–581
Sui	581–618
Tang	618–906
Five Dynasties	907–60
Northern Song	960–1127
Southern Song	1127–1279
Yuan	1271–1368
Ming	1368–1644
Qing	1644–1911

Periods of Military Rule

Kamakura Bakufu	1185–1333
Muromachi Bakufu (Ashikaga Bakufu)	1333–1568
Edo Bakufu (Tokugawa Bakufu)	1603–1867

Battles and Rebellions

❂ Battles

Battle of Inukake	1534
Battles of Konodai	1538, 64
Battles of Kawanakajima	1553–61
Battle of Okehazama	1560
Battles of Sekiyado	1565–74
Battle of Ane River	1570
Battle of Mikatagahara	1572
Battle of Nagashima	1574
Battle of Nagashino	1575
Battle of Shizugatake	1583
Battle of Komakiyama	1584
Battle of Nagakute	1584
Battle of Odawara castle	1590
Battle of Sekigahara	1600
Battle of Dōmyōji	1615

❂ Rebellions

Jinshin Rebellion	672
Hōgen Rebellion	1156
Heiji Rebellion	1159
Jōkyū Rebellion	1221
Genkō Rebellion	1331
Honnō Rebellion	1582
Shimabara Rebellion	1637
Mitō Rebellion	1864–65

 Glossary

ashigaru: Foot soldier.
bokken: Wooden practicing sword.
bokutō: Wooden sword used for practice.
bun-bu: Used to refer to a warrior's civil and martial accomplishments.
daimyō: Feudal lord.
denki: Biography.
deshi: Pupil or desciple of a master of an art or craft who has committed him- or herself to study the art or craft in question for a number of years.
dōjō: Hall with a smooth wooden floor or covered with mats for the practice of martial arts.
go-tairō: Council of Five Regents.
hakama: Trousered skirt, worn by the samurai.
haori: Lightweight silk jacket originally meant to be worn by men as a component of the *hakama*
hatamoto: Direct retainer or "bannerman" of the shogun.
hatasashi: Medieval heraldic banner.
heihō: Art or method of warfare, here generally employed to mean the martial arts, and in particular Musashi's Niten Ichi-ryū.
heihōsha: Practitioner of the art of *heihō*.
hoshu jutsu: Compendium of seizing, holding, and binding techniques that were employed to arrest culprits or deal with those who had been captured alive during siege warfare.
jitte: A traditional weapon consisting of an iron rod that may vary in length between thirty centimeters to a meter with a fork-like extension situated just above the hilt.
jūjutsu: Bare-handed form of combat art based on a variety of grappling techniques.

karusan hakama:	*Hakama* with trouser legs that tapered toward the lower end so that they sat tight round the lower shins.
kataginu:	A stiff sleeveless robe worn by samurai on ceremonial occasions.
kodachi:	Shortest of the pair of swords traditionally worn by samurai.
koku:	Medieval unit of measurement, approximately 180 liters. Here it is used to express the annual rice yield of a plot of land, one *koku* being sufficient to keep a man alive for a year.
kosode:	Generic name for either a lower-class outer garment or an upper-class undergarment.
musha bugyō:	Magistrate of Warriors.
musha shugyō:	Literally, "warrior training" but in the context of *budō*, the old practice of ascetic self-discipline that goes back to the ancient traditions of the so-called *yamabushi*, or enigmatic mountain monks.
naginata:	Pole sword.
omoimono:	Classical Japanese term that can mean either a loved one or a prostitute.
rōnin:	Masterless samurai.
renga:	Series of short verses that are linked into one single poem through a collaborative effort.
ryūha:	A particular branch of a school of swordsmanship
sakuji bugyō:	Administrator responsible for building and repairs.
sashimono:	Medieval heraldic banner.
seppuku:	Ritual suicide.
shaku:	Measure of length, about one foot.
shiai:	Contest between two martial artists.
shidachi:	The junior sparring partner when practicing *kata*. The senior sparring partner is called *shidachi*
shihan:	Chief instructor.

shimenawa:	Lengths of braided rice straw used for ritual purification in Shinto religion.
shinai:	Weapon made of joined segments of bamboo and used in competitive practice.
shinken:	Real sword.
shoshidai:	Deputy governor of the Samurai Dokoro.
shōgun:	Hereditary military governor during Japan's fuedal era.
tachi:	Longest of the pair of swords traditionally worn by samurai.
tantō:	Short dagger.
teppō ashigaru:	*Ashigaru* (foot soldiers) armed with rifles (*teppō*).
uchidachi:	The senior sparring partner when practicing *kata*. The junior sparring partner is called *shidachi*.
wakizashi:	Shortest of the pair of swords traditionally worn by samurai.
yari:	Spear or lance.
yashiki:	Medieval nobleman's mansion.
zōei bugyō:	Construction Magistrate.

 Bibliography

❧ Works in English

Adolphson, Mikael S. *The Gates of Power*. Honolulu, 2000.
—. *The Teeth and Claws of the Buddha*. Honolulu, 2007.
Carroll, John. *Lightning in the Void*. New York, 2006.
Cleary, Thomas. *Code of the Samurai*. Tokyo, 1999.
De Lange, William. *Famous Japanese Swordsmen*, Vols. 1–3. Warren, 2008.
—. *Iaidō*, Boston, 2002.
—. *The Real Musashi: Origins of a Legend, The Bukōden*, Warren, 2011.
—. *The Real Musashi: Origins of a Legend, The Bushū denraiki*, Warren, 2010.
Dening, Walter. *Japan in Days of Yore*. London, 1976.
Friday, Karl F. *Hired Swords*. 1992.
—. *Legacies of the Sword*. 1997.
Hiroaki Satō. *Legends of the Samurai*. New York, 1995.
Jansen, Marius. *Warrior Rule in Japan*. Cambridge, 2008.
Kaufman, Stephen F. *Musashi's Book of Five Rings*. New York, 2004.
Miyamoto Musashi. *The Book of Five Rings*. Translated by Bradford J. Brown. Toronto, 1982.
Miyamoto Musashi. *The Book of Five Rings*. Translated by William Scott Wilson. Tokyo. 2002.
Miyamoto Musashi. *The Book of Five Rings*. Translated by D.E. Tarver. Lincoln, 2002.
Miyamoto Musashi. *The Book of Five Rings*. Translated by Thomas Cleary. Boston, 2000.
Turnbull, S.R. *The Samurai*. New York, 1977.
Sansom, George. *A History of Japan*. Vols 1–3. Tokyo, 1963.
Sato Hiroaki. *Legends of the Samurai*. New York, 1995.
—. *The Sword and the Mind*. New York, 1985.

Sōhō Takuan, *The Unfettered Mind*. Translated by William Scott Wilson. Tokyo, 1986.
Stone, Justin F. *Bushido*. New York, 2001.
Sugawara Makoto. *Lives of Master Swordsmen*. Tokyo, 1982.
Tokitsu Kenji. *Miyamoto Musashi*. Boston, 2005.
Turnbull. S.R. *The Samurai*. New York, 1977.
—. Warriors of Medieval Japan. New York, 2005.
—. *Warriors of Japan*. Honolulu, 1994.
Varley, Paul. *Warriors of Japan*. Honolulu, 1994.
Wilson, William Scott. *Ideals of the Samurai*. Burbank, 1982.
—. *The Lone Samurai*. Tokyo, 2004.
Yamamoto Tsunetomo. *Hagakure*. Translated by William Scott Wilson. Tokyo. 1979.
Yoshikawa Eiji. *Musashi*. Tokyo, 1995.

❧ Works in Japanese

Abe Takeshi. *Sengoku jinmei jiten*. Tokyo, 1990.
Dōmon Fuyuji. *Miyamoto Musashi no jinseikun*. Tokyo, 2000.
Domoto Akihiko. *Kendō kojutsu-shi*. Tokyo, 1988.
Ezaki Junpei. *Nihon kengō retsuden*. Tokyo, 1970.
—. *Yagyū Munenori*. Tokyo, 1971.
Fukuda Akira. *Chūsei katarimono bungei*. Tokyo, 1981.
Fukuda Masahide. *Bushū denraiki*. Tokyo, 2005.
Fukuhara Josen. *Miyamoto Iori no gisho*. Okayama, 1984.
—. *Miyamoto Musashi no tankyū*. Okayama, 1978.
Futaki Kenichi. *Gassen no butaiura*. Tokyo, 1976.
Harada Mukashi. *Shinsetsu Miyamoto Musashi*. Tokyo, 1984.
Hasegawa Shin. *Nihon adauchi isō*. Tokyo, 1974.
Hayashiya Tatsusaburō. *Chūsei geinoshi no kenkyū*. Tokyo, 1960.
Hinatsu Shigetaka. *Honchō bugei shoden*. Tokyo, 2001.
Hioki Shōichi. *Nihon sōhei kenkyū*. Tokyo, 1972.
Hirotani Yūtarō. *Nihon kendō shiryō*. Tokyo, 1943.
Ichikawa Kakuji. *Miyamoto Musashi*. Tokyo, 1985.
Imai Masayuki. *Niten Ichi-ryū seihō*. Tokyo, 1987.
Imamura Yoshio. *Shiryō Yagyū Shinkageryū*. Vols. 1–2. Tokyo, 1995.
—. *Yamato Yagyū ichizoku*. Tokyo, 1974.

Imano Nobuo. *Edo no tabi.* Tokyo, 1986.
Ishioka Hisao. *Hyōhōsha no seikatsu.* Tokyo, 1988.
Kaionji Chōgorō. *Bushō retsuden.* Vols. 1–6. Tokyo, 1964.
Kaku Kōzō. *Miyamoto Musashi jiten.* Tokyo, 2001.
Katsube Mitake. *Bushidō.* Tokyo, 1971.
Kawamura Akira. *Miyamoto Musashi.* Tokyo, 1998.
Kitagawa Hiroshi. *Gunkimono no keifu.* Kyoto, 1985.
Kitajima Matsumoto. *Edo jidai.* Tokyo, 1958.
Kojima Hidehiro. *Kengō densetsu.* Tokyo, 1997.
—. *Sugao no kengōtachi.* Tokyo, 1998.
Kuwata Tadachika. *Chosaku-shū.* Vols. 1–10. Tokyo, 1980.
—. *Nihon no kengō.* Vols. 1–5. Tokyo, 1984.
Maki Hidehiko. *Kengō zenshi.* Tokyo, 2003.
Matsumura Hiroshi. *Rekishi monogatari.* Tokyo, 1979.
Maruoka Muneo. *Miyamoto Musashi meihin shūsei.* Tokyo, 1984.
Matsunobu Ichiji. *Miyamoto Musashi zensho.* Tokyo, 2003.
Miki Seiichirō. *Teppo to sono jisai.* Tokyo, 1981.
Mishima Yukio. *Hagakure nyūmon.* Tokyo, 1967.
Mizuno Yasuo. *Sengoku daimyō Asakurashi to Ichijōdani.* Tokyo, 2002.
Muneta Hiroshi. *Miyamoto Musashi.* Tokyo, 1976.
Nagazumi Yasuaki. *Gunki monogatari no sekai.* Tokyo, 1978.
Nakajima Michiko. *Yagyū Sekishūsai Muneyoshi.* Tokyo, 2003.
Nakamura Akira. *Shinkage-ryū Kamiizumi Nobutsuna.* Tokyo, 2004.
Nakamura Kichiji. *Buke no rekishi.* Tokyo, 1967.
Nakanishi Seizō. *Miyamoto Musashi no saigo.* Tokyo, 1987.
—. *Miyamoto Musashi no Shōgai.* Tokyo, 1975.
Nakayama Hakudō. *Kendō kōwa.* Tokyo, 1937.
Nakazato Kaizan. *Nihon bujutsu shinmyō ki.* Tokyo, 1985.
Nanjō Norio. *Nihon no meijō, kojō jiten.* Tokyo, 1999.
Naoki Sukeyama. *Nihon kengō retsuden.* 1983.
Naramoto Tatsuya. *Bushidō no keifu.* Tokyo, 1973.
—. *Gorin no sho nyūmon.* Tokyo, 1984.
Nishigaya Yasuhiro. *Sengoku daimyō jōkaku jiten.* Tokyo, 1999.
Nitobe Inazo. *Bushidō.* Tokyo, 1938.
Okada Kazuo. *Miyamoto Musashi no subete.* Tokyo, 1983.
Okubō Hikozaemon. *Mikawa Monogatari.* Tokyo, 1980.
Ōmori Nobumasa. *Bujutsu densho no kenkyū.* Tokyo, 1991.

Omori Sōgen. *Sho to Zen*. Tkyo, 1973.
—. *Zen no kōsō*. Tokyo, 1979.
Owada Tetsuo. *Sengoku bushō*. Tokyo, 1981.
—. *Toyotomi Hideyoshi*. Tokyo, 1985.
Ozawa Chikamitsu. *Ken shin itchi*. Tokyo, 1978.
Sakai Tadakutsu. *Sekigahara kassen shimatsu ki*. Tokyo, 1991.
Sasamori Junzo. *Ittō-ryū goku-i*. Tokyo, 1986.
Satome Mitsugu. *Jitsuroku Miyamoto Musashi*. Tokyo, 1989.
Shiba Ryōtarō. *Nihon kenkyaku den*. Tokyo, 1982.
—. *Shinsetsu Miyamoto Musashi*. Tokyo, 1983.
So Dōshin. *Shorinji kenpō*. Tokyo, 1963.
Sugimoto Keizaburō. *Gunki monogatari no sekai*. Tokyo, 1985.
Sukeyama Naoki. *Nihon kengō retsuden*. Tokyo, 1983.
Takahashi tomio. *Bushidō no rekishi*. Vols. 1–3. Tokyo, 1986.
Takano Samirō. *Kendō*. Tokyo, 1915.
Takayanagi Kaneyoshi. *Edo no kakyū bushi*. Tokyo, 1980.
Terada Toru. *Dō no shisō*. Tokyo, 1978.
Terayama Tanchū. *Miyamoto Musashi no ken to bi*. Tokyo, 2002.
Tobe Shinichirō. *Kosho Miyamoto Musashi*. Tokyo, 1984.
Tokutomi Sōho. *Kinsei Nihon kokumin-shi*. Tokyo 1982.
Tominaga Kengō. *Shijitsu Miyamoto Musashi*. Tokyo, 1969.
—. *Nihon gassen zenshū*. Vols. 1–6. Tokyo, 1990.
Watatani Kiyoshi. *Nihon kengō no hyakusen*. Tokyo, 1971.
Watanabe Ichirō. *Budō no meichō*. Tokyo, 1979.
Yabushita Hideki. *Miyamoto Musashi densetsu*. Tokyo, 2001.
Yamazaki Masakazu. *Muromachi ki*. Tokyo, 1974.
Yasuda Motohisa. *Bushi sekai no jōmaku*. Tokyo, 1973.
Yasuda Takashi. *Kata no Nihon bunka*. Tokyo, 1984.
Yokoi Kiyoshi. *Chūsei wo ikita hitobito*. Kyoto, 1981.
Yoshida Seiken. *Nitō-ryū o kataru*. Tokyo, 1941.
Yoshida Yutaka. *Budō hiden sho*. Tokyo, 1973.
—. *Zōhyō monogatari*. Tokyo, 1980.

Index

A
Akamatsu Mochisada (13??–1427) 4, 6–7
Akamatsu Norimura (1277–1350) 6
Akashi castle 79, 85–86
Akiyama Wanao (1618–73) 8, 14, 114
Akizuki castle 4
Amago Hiruhisa (1514–61) 104–105
Amago Katsuhisa (1553–78) 81
Amakusa Shiro 19
Anazawa Morihide 64
Arima Kihei 57
Ashikaga Yoshiaki (1537–97) 35
Ashikaga Yoshiharu (1511–50) 34–35
Ashikaga Yoshimochi (1386–1428) 6–7

B
Bessho Nagaharu (1558–80) 79–81
Bessho Shigeharu (1502–63) 81
Bessho Yoshiko 81
Bisan hōkan xiv, 124–25
Bukōden 8, 14, 35, 48, 77, 84
Bushō kanjō-ki 64
Bushū denraiki 14, 35, 38, 45–46, 48, 56, 67, 75

C
Chikamatsu Shigenori (1697–1778) 82
Chimura Hidenobu 71
Chūjō Nagahide 49

D
Daitoku temple 15
Dōbō goen xiv, 66–68

E
Echigo school of military strategy 100
Edo castle 18, 69
Edōji Sanzuke 110
Emura Sōfu 98
Enmei school of swordsmanship 18, 54, 82, 128

F
Fujiwara no Kintō (966–1041) 81
Fukuyama castle 75, 76
Fukuzumi Dōyō (1626–89) 33, 37
Funage castle 85
Furukawa Koshōken (1726–1807) 88–89

G
Gan school of swordsmanship 31, 46, 93

Ganryū Kojirō. See Sasaki Kojirō
Gaozu (256–195 BC) 22
Gekken sōdan xiii, 17, 91–95, 113, 121–22
Genbō Hideyuki 34
Gifu castle 17
Gikei-ki 61
Gion Tōji 59–60
Godaigo, Emperor (1288–1339) xvi, 6
Gorin no sho xi, xvi, 8, 95, 113, 122
Gotō Mototsugu (1560–1615) 73

H

Han Xin (?–196 BC) 22
Hara castle 19
Harima kagami xiv, 77–81 95, 113
Hassha Jūemon 109
Hayashi Gahō (1618–60) 21
Hayashi Razan (1583–1657) 21, 22, 101, 123
Hayashi Razan bunshū 21
Hayasshi Jussai (1768–1841) 101
Heidaka castle 107
Heidō kagami 17–18, 92–95
Heihō sanjū-go kajō 83–84
Heihō sanjū-kyū kajō 84
Heihō senshi denki 48
Heihōsho 36, 59, 93
Hiezan monastery 129
Hinatsu Shigetaka, (1660–1731) 55–56, 58
Hinatsu Yoshitada (1625–1686) 55

Hirano Yōsai 77–78
Hirata Muni. See Shinmen Muni
Hōkoku shrine 113
Hōkōsho xiii, 39, 115
Honchō bugei shoden xiii–xvi, 55–63, 90, 92, 95, 111, 113–14, 121–22
Honda Masakatsu (1614–1671) 41–42
Honda Masatomo (1599–1638) 41–42
Honda Sakyō 74
Honda Tadakatsu (1548–1610) 126
Honda Tadamasa (1575–1631) 41, 85, 125–26
Honda Tadatoki (1569–1626) 39–42, 115
Honiden Gekinosuke 103–104, 110
Hori Kyōan 71
Hori Sadanori 55
Hōryū temple 78
Hosokawa Tadaoki (1563–1646) 49, 53
Hosokawa Tadatoshi (1586–1641) 32, 50, 54, 65, 84
Hōtō temple 7

I

Ichijō, Emperor (980–1011) 6
Ichijōdani castle 49
Iguchi Nagabei 107
Ikeda Masakoto (1645–1700) 39, 41
Ikeda Mitsumasa (1609–82) 39

Inami gunshi 3
Inga monogatari 24
Ishida Mitsunari (1560–1600) 64, 114, 123
Ishii Mitsunojō 32
Itō Kōnosuke 124
Itō Nagatomo (1764–1850) 89

J

Jiseki gakkō 69
Jūrakudai 36, 38

K

Kaijō monogatari xiv, 24–25
Kami Kagemori 103
Kanemaki Jisai 49
Kanjō shoden. See *Honchō bugei shoden*
Kasahara Kubo 124
Kashiwazaki Eii (17??–1772) 69
Katsuhime (1618–78) 39
Kawagoe Genmi 98
Kawai Kenzaemon 66
Kawasaki Kaginosuke 129
Kawasaki Tokisada 129
Keichō nenchū samurai-chū jija chigyō 105, 109
Keichō shichi-nen shoyakunin chigyōwari 105
Kiichi Hōgen 59, 61
Kinoshita Kyōrin 33
Kinugasa Kurōji 112
Kōkai fūhansō xiii, 45, 50
Kōkō zatsuroku xiv, 71–75
Kokon enkakurō 69
Kokunkan 21, 101

Kokura castle 49
Kokura hibun xiii, xv–xvi, 3, 8–14 35, 48, 56, 95, 111, 114, 123
Konishi Yukinaga (1555–1600) 19
Koro usawa 69
Kōshū school of military strategy 98
Kosuge Ren 124
Kōyō gunkan 55, 101
Kōzuki castle 81
Kumazawa Banzan 64
Kumazawa Itarō 64
Kumoi 66–67
Kunimoto nikki 100
Kuroda Mitsuyuki (1628–1707) 45
Kuroda Nagamasa (1568–1623) 122
Kuroda Yoshitaka (1546–1604) 75, 123
Kurui Ōmi 103
Kyōhachi school of swordsmanship 59, 61

M

Maeda Tsunanori (1643–1724) 51–52
Masaki Teruo 42, 58, 98, 100, 104, 115–16
Matsudaira Hisatada (1697–1742) 71
Matsudaira Katsutaka (1589–1666) 38
Matsudaira Kunzan (1697–1783) 71–72, 74
Matsudaira Naritaka (1788–1838) 99

Matsudaira Naritami (1814–191) 120
Matsudaira Tadahide (1640–?) 62, 63
Matsudaira Tadakuni (1595–1659) 57, 63
Matsudaira Tadanao (1595–1650) 36, 37
Matsudaira Yasuchika (1752–94) 42, 98
Matsudaira Yasunobu (1600–82) 55
Matsudaira Yosritsune (1652–1704) 33
Matsukura Katsuie (1598–1638) 19
Matsura Shigenobu (1622–1703) 64
Mikami Genryū 91, 95
Miki castle 79–81
Mimasaka ryakushi xiv, 58, 95, 120–23
Mimasaka taiheiki 106–107
Minagi Yasuzane 107
Minamoto no Yoshitsune (1159–89) 61
Miyachō Seibei 80
Miyake Gundayū 126, 128
Miyamoto Iori (1612–78) 6, 8, 42, 67, 77–80, 95, 112, 115
Miyamoto Kōhei 39
Miyamoto Kurōemon 118
Miyamoto Kurōtarō 39, 42, 115–16
Miyamoto Mikinosuke (1612–26) 17, 39–41, 112, 115–16, 129

Miyamoto Muni(sai). See Shinmen Muni
Miyamoto Shichirōemon 118
Miyamoto Shume 42, 112, 115–16
Miyamoto Yōemon 116, 117
Mizuno Katsunari (1564–1651) xiv, 15–19, 40, 72–75
Mizuno Katsunari oboegaki 73–74
Mizuno Katsushige (1598–1655) 74
Moji castle 31–32, 54, 65
Mori Naganari (1671–97) 98–99
Mori Nagatake (1645–74) 98
Moriiwa Hikobei 117
Moriiwa Nagataifu 116
Mukashibanashi 82
Murakami, Emperor (926–967) 4, 6
Murasaki Shikibu 6
Musashi Gardens 87
Musashi Meisō Ishi 76
Musō Gonnosuke Katsuyori 24–28, 111

N
Nagano Goroēmon 83–84
Nagao Katsuaki 98, 99
Nakagawa Hidemasa 6
Nakagawa Shimanosuke 17, 40, 76, 115
Nakagawabara castle 17, 115
Nakamura Morikazu 56, 61–62
Nakayama Fumio 75
Nakayama Kageyu 74
Nakayama Shigemori 75–76

Nakayama shrine 120
Nen school of swordsmanship 49
Nenami Okuyama Jion (1351–1427) 49
Nenbutsu jōshi 24
Nihon kendō-shi 129
Nijō castle 52
Niten Ichi school of swordsmanship xvi, 21, 54
Nitenki 48
Numata kaki xiii, 31–32, 50, 90
Numata Nobumoto 31–32

O

Oba Heiba 76
Oba Heizaemon Toshiyuki 15
Obata Kagenori (1572–1663) 55, 101
Oda Nobunaga (1534–82) 49, 51, 81
Odawara castle 69
Ōgaki castle 17
Ogasawara Nagatsugu (1615–66) 67, 116
Ogasawara Tadazane (1596–1667) 4, 24–25, 42, 50, 54, 57, 67, 77, 79, 85–86
Ohara castle 6
Ohara Genshō 5–7, 80
Ohara Nobutada 5
Ohara Nobutoshi 5
Okazaki castle 16
Ono Tadaaki (1565–1628) 51
Osaka castle 19, 39, 42, 73, 75, 85, 115
Osaka join no otomo 76

Osaka o-jin o-ninzu tsukeoboe 76
Osaka ojin no otomo 74–75
Otani Shinsaemon 93

R

Razan sensei isshū 21
Rendai temple 11
Rikan castle 81
Ryūchō monastery 24
Ryūdō temple 103

S

Saitō Denkibō (1550–87) 55
Saiyū zakki 32, 88
Sakaya Seikei (1792–1858) 100–101
Sakuyōshi 98–99
Sanjūrokkasen 80–81
Sasaki Kojirō 31–32, 46–49, 54, 58, 61–65, 88–90, 94, 111, 122
Sawayama castle 114
Sei Shōnagon 6
Seiryūwa 85–86
Sengoku Hidehisa (1552–1614) 40, 42
Senhime (1597–1666) 39
Shiantei 72
Shimazu Yoshihiro (1535–1619) 123
Shimoshō mura kojichō 113–14, 116, 119, 121
Shimoshō mura kojichō-yo 116, 122
Shinmen Higo 109
Shinmen kaki 100, 104–110
Shinmen Munesada 104–105
Shinmen Munetsura 103–110, 121–23

Shinmen Muni 12, 92, 102, 104, 107–110, 118–19, 121
Shinmen Shubei 107
Shinmen Uemon 112, 115
Shintō school of swordsmanship 10
Shoji Jineimon 66
Shoji Katsutomi 66–67
Sieryūwa xiv
Sima Qian (145–86 BC) 22
Sōan Echū (1628–1703) 24
Sōkyūsama o-degatari 15, 92
Sugawara no Michizane (845–903) 5, 7
Sugimoto Yoshichika 51–52
Suzuki Shōsan (1579–1655) 24

T

Tachibana Minehira (1671–1746) 45, 46
Tachibana Shigetane 45–46
Taishō temple 8
Takao Kyūnosuke 112
Takao Magonoshin 112
Takao Magonosuke 112
Takeda school of (mounted) archery 55
Takeda Shingen (1521–73) 51, 98
Takemura Usaemon 53
Takemura Yōemon Yorizumi 54
Takeyama castle 104–105, 108
Tanji Hōkin 67
Tawara Hisamitsu 4, 80
Tawara Iesada 4
Tawara Masahisa 5
Tawara Sadamitsu 4

Tawara Yoshihisa 5
Ten school of swordsmanship 55
Tendō school of swordsmanship 55
Terazawa Hanpei 64
Toda school of swordsmanship 49, 129
Toda Seigen 49, 64, 129
Toda Shigemasa 49
Tōgun school of swordsmanship 128–29
Tōgun Sōjō 129
Tōkōin temple 7
Tokugawa Hidetada (1579–1632) 51–53
Tokugawa Ieyasu (1543–1616) 16, 51, 75, 106
Tokugawa Mitsutomo (1625–1700) 54
Tokugawa Tadanaga (1606–34) 52
Tokugawa Tsugutomo (1692–1731) 71, 82
Tomari jinja munefuda xii, 3, 39, 80, 95, 114–15
Tomari shrine 4, 79–80
Tomida castle 105
Tomohira Shinnō (964–1009) 3, 6
Tōsakushi xvi, 42, 58, 95, 98–123
Toyotomi Hidetsugu (1568–95) 38
Toyotomi Hideyori (1593–1615)
Toyotomi Hideyoshi (1537–98) 16, 38, 64, 69, 81
Tsuyama castle 120

U
Ueda castle 51
Ueda Sōnyū. See Sasaki Kojirō
Uehara Sakon 107
Ukita Hideie (1572–1655) 105–106, 113, 123
Ukita Naoie (1529–82) 105–106

W
Watanabe Kōan 51, 52–54
Watanabe Kōan taiwa-ki 51–54

Y
Yabuki Masanori (1833–1906) 120
Yagyū Munenori (1571–1648) 51, 53
Yagyū Shinkage school of swordsmanship 52, 54, 83
Yahazu castle 107
Yamaga school of military strategy 100
Yamaga Sokō (1622–85) 21, 100–101
Yamazaki Rokusaemon. See Toda Shigemasa
Yasuhigashi Gensaemon 107
Yoshiaki Shinnō (904–37) 6
Yoshiaki, Emperor (1537–97) 12
Yoshikawa Eiji (1892–1962) 74–75, 109
Yoshioka Naoshige 11, 35, 37
Yoshioka Kanefusa 69–70
Yoshioka Kenpō 61, 64, 93, 122
Yoshioka Matashichirō 11
Yoshioka Naokata 34
Yoshioka Naomitsu 34, 36
Yoshioka Naomoto 34, 35
Yoshioka school of swordsmanship 12, 34, 35
Yoshioka Naotsuna 11, 35–37, 72
Yoshioka-den xiii, 19, 33–38
Yūki Hideyasu (1574–1607) 37

TOYO Press publishes books that contribute to a deeper understanding of Asian cultures. Editorial supervision: Ray Furse. Book and cover design: Keichō Designs. Printing and binding: IngramSpark. The typefaces used are Cochin and Cochin Archaic.

www.ingramcontent.com/pod-product-compliance
Lightning Source LLC
Chambersburg PA
CBHW071452080526
44587CB00014B/2074